Natural
Resonance

GLIDDEN BOOKS
WWW.GLIDDENBOOKS.COM

Dedication

To my inner circle;
with whom I vibe with
synergy.

Infinite gratitude .

XOXO

Table of Contents

Introduction

"*Love in the past is only a memory. Love in the future is only a fantasy. True love lives in the here and now.*"

–Buddha

It's the little thoughts that change us bit by bit every day. Electrically, the information of our thoughts grow, join with other ideas, and combine into our coherent psyche. In other words, it is thoughts that power our brains, run our bodies, and orient us with the world. From our unique interpretations of the world, we form an inner understanding from which our subsequent thoughts, behaviors, and actions radiate back into the populous through our interaction with it.

The recurrent thoughts and questions that we gravitate towards shaping us into who we are in application. This natural cause and effect is a beautiful process; however, it's very easy for other ideas that aren't ours to creep in and take hold. By slowing down and taking the time that it takes to examine the beliefs that sustain us, we open ourselves to key transformations that elevate our experience of life. Essentially, we excavate the mind to ensure that we're operating from a space of our own gravitational and interpretive authenticity.

May you never believe the lie that you must hide parts of yourself in exchange for acceptance. Every single, layered, complicated piece of you lends beauty and wholeness to your being. You don't need to adopt anyone else's way of thinking or being. It's okay to be you.

Natural Resonance is a collection of everyday thoughts and questions that encourage us to slow down and to reconsider the simple things that, when mindfully received, can help us evolve into who we are becoming. We are always becoming a different version of ourselves. When we remember how to stand up as a representative of our totality and wholeness, we are the embodiment of cosmic vitality.

In the disciplines of yoga, to "yoke" is to unify, cultivate, and integrate all things which amalgamate into life, as it is uniquely expressed through us as individuals that are part of a populous of separate entities.

As an individual, you are a tapestry, a canvas upon which life's many layers are represented as one unique person; you. In the words and concepts that I've included here, I hope that you find support in untangling the tiny things that build up, trip us up, and require us to tease out and reweave our personal stories through a loving routine of gentle interior maintenance.

We are cosmic atoms manifest on Earth for a temporary experience in a coherent physical body; in anima our awareness is the gateway for spiritual exploration. As we experience transitions through life, these spiritual journeys are personal, complex, and always evolving.

In acknowledging the reality that we each choose to go about investigating and healing via different routes and practices, I have tried to make my words universally applicable to compliment your belief system, whatever that may be. As you make your way through these pages, I hope that you will receive all concepts, questions, and statements in the same way: with genuine discernment.

Whatever it is, Just let it land.

Observe how it affects you,

what it makes you think of,

how it makes you feel.

See what fits.

Release the rest.

It is understood we all encounter events of dysfunction, pain, and suffering at some point that instinctively spark our base impulse to withdraw, retract and shy away from the awe of the world in an attempt at self-preservation. When this happens, we often take shelter in adopting coping skills, reasoning, and behavioral strategies supported by a larger social group; our tribe, if you will. This assimilation is effective in the short-term. Yet, when we fail to revisit themes and stimulus when we have re-rooted into safety, we migrate farther and farther away from the lessons and sentiment that our individuated anima requires to grow and evolve.

In this text, I intend to comfort you, inspire you, and encourage you to rethink your current perception of life themes that affect your vital energies, as often and as many times as your deem necessary. These are gentle, loving reminders to put you back in touch with who you are, and what's at stake for you in this life. I hope that you allow these phrases to create a series of sacred space within yourself, where all that you've encountered before this moment at hand, can be revisited, recategorized, and refined into usable material for your forward moving progression.

In these sacred spaces of self-appraisal and soul searching, we witness our former selves dying (metaphorically, of course) as we open up to regeneration. From this space of intellectual reorganization, we revitalize our psyche. We learn to form and reform ourselves repeatedly as we change with the tides of life.

Here, deep inside ourselves, we discover our abilities to meet and greet our divinity and to excavate the strength and fortitude to meet the world as it is, on our terms. We discover that even the disliked experiences are part of the migrative journey; they add something vital to our story.

A lot of my work centers around the conceptual and tangible expressions of faith. Everyone encounters times of deep questioning regarding their faith, themselves, and the choices that they make. Whatever it is that we believe or reject plays a role in our inner narrative. Additionally, those beliefs interact with the changing tenants of the world at large. This interaction between both our conscious & subconscious beliefs steer our choices for how we manifest our thoughts and behaviors in society.

Disconnects in our life, minds, and bodies assist us in identifying and updating what needs mending. These are the life elements that will ultimately enable us to build the bridges and gateways back to vibrant, full, authentic lives. Part of this is done by unearthing our connections to faith (in various forms), again and again.

It is a fundamental part of our human nature to question things, especially when encountering incongruencies, injustices, and suffering. So, that's what I want you to do; question things and see what you uncover.

One of the best services that we can provide ourselves with is to lean into what resonates with the personal truth that we carry.

Human languages ascribe various words and cultural connotations to all acts and processes of living. Be assured that we are all still traveling the same divine path of being, even if our words, beliefs, and customs aren't necessarily reflective of that.

As we experience the physical densities of life and strive to take it all in and organize it into a coherent baseline from which we can navigate our realities, all information is subject to varied interpretation. We live here as fleshy beings, animated by spirit, experiencing many similar things from wildly varied viewpoints.

Universally, behind all other goals and desires, we instinctively yearn for safety, social harmony and the warmth of sustenance.

May you unearth the truth that peace isn't found by aligning with the value judgments of the outside world but rather, in embracing the manifestations of our being in alignment with the spirit energy that flows from within us and back out into the world.

To find our truth is awareness.

Living that truth is alignment.

In routinely returning our awareness to our personal truths, we observe our miraculous ability to evolve and thrive, no matter what we externally encounter.

Meditation is an incredible tool for opening the mind to transformation. Arising out of that, the ego is quieted long enough for us to hear the resonant whispers of our spirit and to connect us directly with divinity. There, no answers, solutions or possibilities are out of reach.

In yoking, we mindfully connect to all kinds of energies in the receipt, application, and perpetuation of love, peace, and innate wisdom. The light of knowing flows freely, ripples up, energizes us, and vibrates back out into the world with resonant refinement.

From the inside out, we connect, evolve, and eventually find whatever we are attracting and seeking. When humbled by life, we can return to what resonates as true.

All revelations are correct for the individuals that they appeal and apply to. Mindfully seeking, we uncover our deepest truths within the safe confines of our evolving worldview. Image how you will emerge on the other side of the path that you are on today.

Make moments each day to connect with yourself, with your light, and with your inner knowing. Let the pure magic of reflection allow you to embrace the beautiful life that you are already living.

Contemplate, experience, and fully unwrap the sacred journey that thrives within you. For now, we yoke. May your adventures be full of light, love, and levity.

-Meg

Natural
Resonance

Through the door of the womb,
we arrive into being.

Across time,
we are wandering through life like gypsies along an
unmarked path.

Be here fully.
Feel grounded in the flesh.
Rejoice in the abundance of the senses.

All life shares a singular pulse.
In nature, we find our inherent flow.
Take a breath and connect with yours.

Embrace the rhythms that usher you forward.

Be ever-curious, and walk where you are yearning to
go.

Intention manifests delight.

When in doubt,
do not hesitate to reach through the universe,
across all barriers and down the rabbit hole
to find the truths that you seek.

Let the mark you impress cause no pain.
You are pivotal without trying to be.
Take heed of this.

When one tries too hard,
there is pain, where only surrender was needed.
In kindness, be bold and brilliant.

With faith,
peace will deliver you where you most need to go.

Above all, be love.
Weave every thread of your life with care.
Prepare to stretch and bend without damage.
Let friends strengthen you through connection.
Act always with honest intent.

Share every joy with courage.

What Is Resonance?

EVERYTHING vibrates,

all the way down to the atom.

Do you know that, as of 2020, the average human attention span is only about 8 seconds long? 8 seconds...how much can we learn, observe, or connect to in such a short time? Do you know that that number has shortened with the advancement of technology? It's interesting how we evolve or devolve based on our behaviors' conditioning in response to the current commonalities of life. How important do we value our attention to be? Sometimes, 8 seconds might be all it takes to take in what we need and move on, but I believe wholeheartedly that there are many times when it's important to allow attention to linger. Connection takes longer than 8 seconds. Day by day we must steer ourselves back from such a reactionary relationship with life.

In yoga, we learn to quiet, strengthen, and honor the mind-body in ways that regularly result in lengthening and expanding our abilities to be present in any given moment. As we progress, we can retain one-pointed focus (aka hold our attention) much longer when we mindfully intend ourselves to do so. With that in mind, I have designed this text to accommodate our ability to absorb ourselves in rich and focused ways and accept that some days, we simply shift back to our default '8 seconds'.

To meet ourselves where we are, we must accept that some days we need a rich, nourishing lesson, other days we need only a drop of inspiration, and at some times, only a meditation that helps us travel within will do. SO, let's take the first step in linking together some incredible information to assist you on your peaceful, aware, and well informed, mind-body journey.

There are many sciences of sound and vibration. I myself, am not a scientist of sound, only a loving observer of it. In this life, I am formally educated in mental health and yoga, each affecting the mind-body relationship. I mean, that's pretty much the real point for both fields isn't it? To understand enough to cultivate a prime quality of life in application. In usage, both frequently send me searching for information and answers that cross over into spectrums of other sciences, philosophies, and practices.

In my studies, I wanted to know, "What if we could draw our awareness to these subtle energetic exchanges and tune in enough to observe what types of resonance are taking place?"

It stands to reason that when we attune to resonance, it becomes easier to identify vibrations that are not in-line with our wants, needs and values sets. Thus, easier to free up the space and energy we need to mindfully seek the vibrations that strike our natural predilections in a complimentary way instead. For example, when people say, "that resonated with me", they are consciously describing a vibrational match with a stimulus , whoever/whatever it is/was. Incredibly, the results of this are visible to scholars in the field of Psychoacoustics, which tracks how sound influences our nervous system. The study of visible sound wave interaction and transformations is called Cymatics. Research in these areas are brimming with information on how vibrations affect and transform every layer of being.

For a simplistic, person-centered reference, just take a moment and think about how different tones or types of music evoke different postures, thoughts, and emotional responses in your body. Notice how various tones impact your mind-body in alternative ways. The science of sound, is not a woo-woo concept. In physics, they call it the study of Acoustics. In application, they call it acoustical engineering. Within the context of Yogic and Ayurvedic lifestyle practices, these elements are considered part of your energetic diet. They are a facet of recurrent stimulus that influences the mind-body through exposure and intake. To accommodate for this, it helps to understand it, at least a little.

Our energetic diet begins within us; in the thoughts, emotions, and patterns that we choose to maintain. "We are electrical beings; our bodies generate electricity and depend on it for survival. (Dale, 2009)." Flows of electricity, produce magnetic fields. As they come together as a single entity, every layer of our bodies create both bioelectrical and bio-magnetic fields that resonate as a closed system that both influences and is influenced by inner and external stimulus.

'Resonance' is a word used to describe a natural vibrational match.

The next time someone suggests that you "raise your vibration," I want you to think about this; continual energetic vibrations are thrumming around and within us at all times. When natural vibrational matches interact, they sync up, knocking out any minor distortions and restoring natural resonance. This healthy vibrational resonance interaction is described as 'entrained' and illustrates an organically baseline, harmonious state.

In our interactions with the external world, stronger vibrations can move in and cause our energy to shift out of our natural frequency. These externally forced changes are called 'entrainment' and mean that the natural baseline is being conditioned into another vibration state. These disruptions can be positive or negative; 'coherent' or 'dissonant'. Coherency is considered positive as it holds the potential to elevate, evolve, or in some way improve the original resonance. Dissonance is negative because it causes imbalanced, discordant reactions.

Physical dissonance gives rise to sickness. Cognitive dissonance produces inconsistencies of mind (thought patterns) that create extenuating problems with emotions and behaviors that disrupt intra and interpersonal relationships.

Vibrations impact us like a dial.

We can consciously turn our exposure to vibrations up or down both inside and outside our physical being. At birth, we arrived in this life with a naturally resonant vibration that is continually impacted and altered from that juncture onward. Basically, that dial has been moving, being cranked up and dialed down over and over ever since we took our first breath. We feed, experience, grow, and change in response to the fluid stream of life stimulus.

To illustrate some of this information a little better, let's think about our common interactions with emotions. We all have them, we're all subject to fluctuations within them daily, and yet, we also know that what prompts certain emotional responses in one person, can differ greatly from the response it evokes in another. Our life experiences have conditioned us each in different ways. When an internal emotional vibration is sparked (due to any internal or external event), the mind, body, and vibration strike up in reaction to the change. Think of the feeling of joy and observe your reaction. Now, think of sadness... There is a physical, mental, emotional, and vibrational system of changes in response to both. It just is, and whatever your initial reaction to both was just now, it is a conditioned response in all layers. Your responses are considered 'conditioned' ones, because as we age, our historical account of mind-body-emotion reactions develops following whatever it is that we have previously experienced, playing out into the current moment.

The energetic movement of emotion in particular, is a great illustrator of the mind-body-vibrational connections.

Heightened emotion usually shuts down the more logical portions of our brain ('when we're feeling, we're not thinking' because our ability for logic is reduced. Our logic energy is re-routed to provide fuel for the experience of the emotion. Remember, our physical bodies are intuitive electrical systems that are hardwired to preserve themselves without shorting out. We can't do everything at once).

There are pivotal differences between consciously embracing emotions, and being in an active, emotionally reactive state.

When we are consciously embracing our emotions (such as when we are meditating or witnessing thoughts and emotions), our emotional energy does not exist in a heightened state. Thus, our brain's logical parts are still online and actively working in unison with our other biological and energetic systems.

In emotional responses to themes and stimulus that incite our survival responses to kick in, there are 4 preformatted responses in the human psyche: Fight, Flight, Freeze, and Fawn. Each sends out its own vibrational resonance.

Fight - Resist

Flight - Flee

Freeze - Immobilization

Fawn - Appease and avoid conflict

Life happens. If an external emotional vibration comes in and it is upset or angry, it sweeps over us and affects the mind-body in a dissonant way. Conversely, when an energetic burst or joy vibrates into a room, all of the vibrational frequencies that it encounters are subsequently altered by it. In short, our cellular vibrational composition continually interacts with the vibrations around us, without discernment. This is a cosmic happening.

As the universal hums of space are audible in the farthest reaches of the universe, the same hums and variances apply within us. Perhaps you've heard the Hermetic axion, "As within, so without." Within this saying, it becomes understood that as we build our ability to observe the world within and around us (the microcosm), refining it, cleaning it up, and honoring it, we influentially alter the macrocosm (larger world, universe, etc) as well. In the following passage, Suzy Kassem captures the essence of this relationship beautifully:

"MUSIC OF THE UNIVERSE

> *Without the orchestra of the universe,*
>
> *There would be no ether.*
>
> *And without its instrumentation*
>
> *By the ether,*
>
> *There would be no waves.*
>
> *And without any waves,*
>
> *There would be no sound.*
>
> *And without sound,*
>
> *There would be no music.*

And without music,

There would be no life.

And without a life force,

There would be no matter.

But it does not matter -

Because what is matter,

If there is no light?"

-From Rise Up and Salute the Sun: The Writings of Suzy Kassem

When we step outside of the idea of a dualistic universe and embrace the idea that all parts equally and aspects of life facilitate innate wholeness, we open up and soften a little more to the intricacies that flow inseparable to being. Sound vibration is the foundational.

As birds and bacteria react to changes in the Earth's magnetic field, they are responding to the changes of vibration. In 'real' life, ever, day, the nuance of most of these interactions are overshadowed by the louder, more catchy thoughts, emotions, and happenings that are easier for us to spot and maneuver. However, this can help and harm our efforts to maintain balance in a Sattvic (calm, harmonious) way.

When we ignore vibrational changes, we miss important cues to alter our thoughts and behaviors in the most harmonious way. Through resonance with every stimulation, vibrations are amplified, for the better, or sometimes, for the worse. In a way, bringing our attention back to this attunement to vibration, asks us to tap back into our basic animal instincts; can we restore our sensing of natural vibrations, and apply this information consciously?

Under the microscope the unseen ebbs and flows.

Beneath what's visible, your anatomical makeup reacts too, through invisible changes in their electrical frequency.

In the body, dense tissues, like our spinal column and other bodily systems, act as our conduits of information, running energy and electric information through our bodies and to our brain in loops. Stimulus, like conversations, aromatic flowers, or the sensations of a fire, or cool wind, are experienced from the body's seat and relayed back into the brain. Once the sensory stimulus arrives the brain is tasked to make sense of what has just been input into the data-stream of our personal experience.

This information is measured against our brains historical records, and then synthesized for systemic organization, which results in subsequent thoughts, emotions and reactions. In this way, resonance directly influences our orientation to the world. Over time, as a matter of efficiency, our brains will automatically resonate with or repel certain data sets based on our personal history.

To upgrade our patterns and responses, we must actively recondition our brains so that our problematic automatic responses are negated and replaced by what we consciously prefer.

Scientifically, we know more about the world and the integrative mechanics of brain, body, and systems that ever before. Socially, mainstream society chooses to casually ignore every bit of verifiable phenomenon that our predecessors strived ceaselessly to investigate. It's a bit ironic, but perhaps that's part of some collective samskara (karmic impression) that we all must navigate in this life. Within the construct of our physical bodies, what will we do with 'more information'?

For generations, humanity was steeped in tradition and philosophies that honored connectedness. Then, as technologies evolved, the collective purview shifted focus towards quantifying and validating the unknown. Once they did and their revelations successfully landed in the next generation's lap, most people didn't care anymore about discoveries' mechanics.

They just use them without a second thought.

Unfortunately, this mindless usage attitude also drowned out what lingered of our connection to philosophy, which is, simply put, the underlying framework of eternal linkage (human, nature, and cosmos). What if that wasn't a trade that we had to make? Would you take the time that it takes to shift back into a more natural state of being?

Maybe today is a great day for each individual to ask themselves new questions. To turn the dial back and tune in to the subtle, infinite connection. It's there, and it's waiting for you to make yourself available.

How do we reintegrate the aware, connected traditions of living with the technology that yielded unparalleled knowledge and simultaneously introduced a general, widespread numbness that wrapped the world in distractions?

The answer is, "One individual at a time." That's the way that we heal self and inspire the world. It may not be super expedient, but it is incredibly effective.

Given power, impatience creates discord in experience. Cosmic vibration hurries not for the ego.

You are not a slave to your nature; you're the conscious conductor of it.' Knowing' is just the independent awareness of what is going on around us, and within us. In repetitive noticing, we marry these two things in the full, embodied expression of our inner knowing. We mustn't rush, but instead recondition ourselves not to scurry.

Long before it was in vogue to 'be woke', the philosophies of ancient human civilizations captured the vital essence of connection, and we can too.

From a space of deeply seated awareness, we can honor and uphold the sacred pact of being. We begin by lining out and examining what we believe, why we believe it, and alter our daily life choices to match our inner convictions, we serve ourselves by evolving into more coherent, synergistic, authentic human beings.

Start with creating some space, slowing down, and breathing in moments of quiet. Gravitate toward stimulus, thoughts, and practices that resonate with you. Identify what questions that you really want to ask.

• What if, instead of latching on to self-perpetuating hate and fears of social disturbance, we honored the values of our single human heritage?

• Could we instead pay homage to the incredible growth and opportunity within our reach as a collective humanity today?

• What if we could pause long enough to connect and lean into that?

• What if living with modern convenience didn't require us to trade our actual, resonant reality of connectedness?

• How can we evolve to heal the wounds of humanity for the greater good?

"We must be willing to get rid of the life we've planned, so as to have the life that is waiting for us. The old skin has to be shed before the new one can come."

—Joseph Campbell

THIS IS A

Beginning

This is a Beginning

Daily, our inner spirits have a unique need for nourishment, and we often start out seeking that in the ordinary stories of the world.

We don't find sustainable nourishment there, outside of ourselves, because our story often transcends the familiar narratives that we encounter in the world. When we are in the states of questioning, seeking, and evolving who we are, we have to learn to honor that and reconcile the ordinary and non-ordinary. As an individual, I love to learn and share information to increase my experience and understanding of both the individual and broader levels. On occasion, I create things from a deeply seated source of inspiration and put it out into the world for anyone who may need it.

Psychologically, all of us have at least one origin story of which we are aware of. Usually, we have several that thread together and get built upon year after year. These narrative tales are our baseline stories that pinpoint how, what, when, and where something began. All things in this physical world are highly susceptible to fallibilities in perception.

We interpret the world through verbalization, memory, and gradually changing interpretations, all of which are migratory. Within these reflections, I hope you learn to edit your stories where they are outdated and learn to serve yourself best by letting go of what no longer serves you.

Forgive yourself.

Let go of futile hope for a better past.

Begin anew today.

Hold sincere gratitude for NOW.

Right now is all the time we've got.

Every day, we have a million opportunities to learn new ways to heal and grow from the inside out. Each morning is an awakening. Let the slightly evolved version of yourself free. Just for that day, allow that miraculous version of yourself to be enough. Allow each slightly healed aspect of yourself to empower you to overcome all that is yours to transcend.

All the little things you capture in a day, over a week, for a year; The snippets of thoughts, quotes, and ideas that catch your attention, however momentary, are part of your experience. They are more important than we give them credit for. Their value is our responsibility. Will we let them build us up, blind us to the truth, or sway us upon the path we are working towards?

In this lifetime, we will each speak over 860 million words, each full of resonance of all kinds. Some will count; many won't. We scatter the air with the vibrations of words that lift us and thrill us, stories that bring us down, and some that cause injury to others. Instantly forgotten conversations waft around like wind, and some sacred few lands heavily upon the Earth and stay with us forever as ingrained vibrational marks upon our being.

The essential words are the words that vibrate with a resonance that feels like home. The messages that connect you to yourself, to spirit, and carry you into connection or disconnection with others. Even more important than the words themselves is the silence between them. That's the energy that breathes life and wisdom into all. The better that we can become at isolating, cultivating, and perpetuating these lasting vibrations of truth and love, the more peace we can shower upon the world, built of the pure cosmic love that churns within us in anima.

All people are fallible creatures. We all get confused, lost, and drunk on ego from time to time. While it is true that people often miscommunicate the workings of the spirit, it is not an absolute truth that all structures for praise and worship are corrupt. Find your way to honor your divinity and allow that to be enough to fill you up and sustain you.

There are many things about the origins of life that we do not understand, but all of those gaps considered, there is so much useful information that we DO have, that there are no excuses left to bypass spirit. While the human mind is predisposed to specific patterns of thinking & behaving and holds a preference for order, routine, and conditioning, our energy is far more resilient and robust than we frequently give it credit for. We are incredible creatures primed for continual evolution. Together, we explore, examine and search for what resonates.

If you so choose, this is a beginning.

Of What?!

I have no idea.

It's totally up to YOU.

WHAT WITHIN YOU IS READY TO MANIFEST?
WHAT DO YOU WANT TO ANIMATE FROM WITHIN
AND EMANATE OUTWARD INTO BEING?

Extraordinary Warrior

YOU ARE CAPABLE
OF RISING TRIUMPHANTLY ANY BATTLE.

SOFTEN TO THE CRUSADES THAT YOU MEET.
ENSURE THAT YOUR EVERY CAMPAIGN ALIGNS
WITH YOUR INNER WISDOM.

WHEN YOU ARE ABLE,
FORGO STRUGGLE ENTIRELY.

CHOOSE FIRST
THE AVAILABLE PATHS OF PEACE,
BUT WHEN YOU MUST FIGHT,
KNOW INTIMATELY THE VIRTUOUS QUALITIES
STEWARDING YOUR CAUSE AHEAD.

Our connectedness to
life is tied to the depths
of our connectedness to
the entirety of self.

INVITE THE BODY TO RELEASE EVERY TENSION
FROM THE FIBERS OF YOUR BEING.

In our partnership with the dense physical animation of the body, the mind is aware that it is conscious, and that it can power ripples of energy from the body and effect the world.

WHERE DO YOU WANT TO SEND YOUR ENERGY?
WHAT DO YOU WANT TO MAKE AN EFFECT ON?

Allow yourself the
adventure of exploring
the mind-body with love,
stillness, and curiosity.

INVITE THE SWEET NECTAR OF BREATH TO FILL
YOUR LUNGS WITH AIR.

The greatest wonder of this awareness is in the infinite potential to accept yourself, others, life, and knowledge fully, right where you are.

You are already perfect,
innately connected.

BE HERE

Sink in deep.
Watch the sweet sun
rise and set.
Embrace each moment,
as if it were a precious,
passing novelty.

How we understand and express the sum of our experiences in this life, is our own, individual responsibility.

Rhythmically, we discern, integrate, and evolve in all the quiet recesses of our being.

The status quo is nothing but a comfy figment of the imagination.

PREFERENCE OFTEN PILFERS PROGRESSION.

What if trust has less to do with anyone else and everything to do with the ability to cultivate and hold self-confidence and faith in your own integrity?

CAN YOU CULTIVATE TOTAL SELF-TRUST THAT DOESN'T FALTER AGAINST THE TREATMENT OF OTHERS?

Don't let the ego resist
what Divinity has
designed.

PRACTICE ALLOWING.

Accept.

Center.

Evolve.

A.C.E. TRANSITIONS.
AKA GO WITH THE FLOW

No use lingering in the
how's and why's of
shame and blame.

WHEN LIFE IS SIGNALING YOU TO SHIFT,
CORRECT COURSE AND SAIL ON WITHOUT
BAGGAGE.

Observe Your Own Inner Light

ALLOW YOUR WITNESS TO STRENGTHEN.
UNLEASH HER INTO EVERY INNER SPACE WHERE
THE EGO WAILS TO RUNS RIOT.

Open Up

BEING OPEN LETS MIRACLES IN.
WE WANT THAT DON'T WE?

Answer the call to share your
sacred gifts & blessings.
Forget not your hallowed purpose.
Explore the world with might.

THROUGH THE DOOR OF THE
WOMB, WE ARRIVE INTO
BEING. ACROSS TIME, WE EMERGE
INTO REALITY AS VARIOUS FORMS
AND VISIONS OF THAT FROM
WHICH WE SPRANG.

THIS IS EXISTENCE

LEARN TO BE HERE FULLY.

EXIST LOVINGLY, THOUGHTFULLY,
AND WITH INNATE GRATITUDE.

WE MUSTN'T RUSH THE MIRACLE TO FRUITION.

ALL WILL TRANSPIRE IN INTUITIVE TIME.

REJOICE IN THE ABUNDANCE OF LIFE AS IT
APPEARS IN THE NOW.

AFTER ALL, YOU, TOO,
ARE A BLOSSOM OF DIVINE LOVE.

Totally In Tact

YOU ARE ALWAYS INTACT.

WE HEAR AND SEE SUCH A LOW PERCENTAGE OF
THE EXISTING AUDITORY AND VISUAL
LANDSCAPE THAT IT STARKLY LIMITS OUR
CONCEPTIONS OF REALITY AS IT TRULY IS. FOR
CREATURES WHO LIVE THEIR ENTIRE LIVES
DEPENDENT ON THE STIMULATION LIMITED TO
THE FIVE PRIMARY SENSES, THIS IS A MOMENT
TO STOP, SLOW DOWN, AND THINK ABOUT THAT
FOR A SECOND.

IN WHAT WAYS DUE TO OUR LIMITED
CAPABILITIES NARROW OUR CONCEPTION OF
THE WORLD AS WE KNOW IT?

CAN YOU ACCEPT THAT YOU ARE WHOLE, AS
WELL AS A WORK IN PROGRESS,
SIMULTANEOUSLY?

Greet the Days

TASKS AND TOILS OFT PRESENT THEMSELVES IN
LITANY, YET THESE ARE LESS ADVERSARY TO
THOSE WHO CAN SINK INTO ACCEPTANCE.

JOURNEYING IS THE WORK OF BEING; A
WILLINGNESS TO ACKNOWLEDGE THE LIMITS OF
THE WILL, SO THAT THE WONDER HAS ROOM TO
WORK THROUGH US.

TO TOUR THE WORLD WITH WONDER AND
GRACE, IS A PATH OF GREETING EVERY
OBSTACLE AS THE OPPORTUNITY THAT IT
EMANATES.

THERE IS POETRY IN
BEING

Connected

How Do I Get Connected?

*"Be willing to be a beginner
every single morning."*
—Meister Eckhart

Connection is how we gauge what is going on. When we are disconnected, it's easier to run ourselves ragged (mind, body, and spirit) because all of those subtle unseen things are playing out, totally unchecked. It is the gateway to our relationship with life and everything in it.

Why Does It Work So Well?

Taking the time to establish an intentional focus on the various layers of our lives provides the feedback we relay to our brain. The brain is the real 'reality' checker. But sometimes, it needs tuning up.

Feedback is THE tool for connection and self-regulation. Whether we consciously want to change or accept something new or not, feedback is a balancing mechanism.

Our body tells us things, as does our gut instinct, our relationships, and the reaction that we are receiving when we levy our will out into life. It wakes our autopilot systems up and suggests edits and modifications.

Without connection and feedback, we will go on forever, operating naturally in our environment without any checks and balances. During prolonged periods of extreme isolation, human beings suffer in a myriad of ways.

Feedback corrects processes that would otherwise go unnoticed, unchallenged, and even avoided in our preference to maintain the comfy status quo that we often fall into. Since connection encourages feedback, we can allow this relationship to work it's magic intentionally. Through nourishing the bonds of feedback, we find more information than we can give to ourselves.

Self-Connection Is Self-care.

We want to take care of ourselves. The thing is, any imbalances, disruptions, and discord require our attention. Without being observed, with intentional attention, how will you know what to nurture and mend?

You can't correct something that you are unaware of. The human brain is a Master of Systems and processes. Over time, our habits and tendencies hardwire our thought, emotional, and behavioral patterns. When the subconscious determines that a particular way of being is the most efficient, it drops all the neural pathways for doing it a different way. The brain says, "we can forget this." Therefore, in the tasks of daily living (including communication), we naturally get set onto ""autopilot"" until something disrupts the efficiency of what we're doing.

Community connection is important.

What is it about the magic of connection with our community members that we so often overlook it?

When we want to connect with ourselves, we have to open to relationships. Within the reciprocity of social interaction, there is an incredible amount of feedback, support, and encouragement.

Socialization is more than leisure. The beauty of connection is that it is a wellspring of joy, exchange, and a humbling reminder that life isn't only about us. Through connecting, we grow and learn to expand our current capabilities of love. Community is the gift of society, but only if we can wade through the muck and connect with all the love and possibility that exists.

Most of us are in contact with other people regularly. And yet, how often do you connect?

I'm not talking about acquaintances or business contacts here, I'm talking about people that resonate with you. How often do you interact with people who get to experience you without any pretense of defense in place? What percentage of that time is spent in an undistracted, fully connected kind of way?

Participation in groups of people is an essential part of an informed, individual evolution. Social groups foster the strengthening of supportive communities and encourage feedback amongst members. Besides love and camaraderie, this feedback is our social interaction, 'takeaway.' It can be a thought, a feeling, or information, but it is vitally important in whatever form it takes. Whether perceived as positive or negative, this feedback wields the incredible ability to provide the relevant, up to date input that we need to self-evaluate honestly.

From ethereal source springs opportunity.

YOU ARE A LIVING, BREATHING MIRACLE.

One Day, We Realize,

NO MATTER THE CRISIS, ARGUMENT, OR
PERCEIVED PROBLEM AT HAND;

WE DECAY UNTIL WE GROW.
WE ISOLATE UNTIL WE OPEN.
WE CHOOSE THE PARALYSIS OF RIGIDITY,
UNTIL WE CAN REMEMBER HOW TO BE OPEN AND
SOFT AGAIN.

My Work is to identify what is for me

AND TO LET GO OF WHAT BELONGS TO OTHERS.

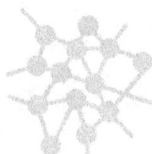

Life is more than moving from point A to point B.

BEING ISN'T STATIC,
EVEN WHILST AT REST.

WHEN IT APPEARS THAT 'NOTHING' IS
HAPPENING, TAKE SOLACE IN KNOWING THAT
SUBTLE FUNCTIONS ARE STILL MAKING
HEADWAY.

Our connectedness to
life is tied to the depths
of our connectedness to
the entirety of self.

INVITE THE BODY TO RELEASE EVERY TENSION
FROM THE FIBERS OF YOUR BEING.

Soul Assist

DO YOU NEED ONE?

BLESSED. WE ARE BLESSED; ME, YOU,
EVERYTHING, AND EVERYONE THAT YOU TOUCH
AND SEE.

HOW CAN YOU HONOR THAT TODAY?

IN THIS LIFE, OUR SOULS JOURNEY THROUGH
TRIUMPH AND LOSS, PLEASURE AND PAIN,
AGING, AND TRANSFORMATION ARE PART OF THE
FULL CIRCLE EXPERIENCE.

SHARING IS AN EXPRESSION OF VULNERABILITY,
JUST AS RECEIVING IS ITS DIVINE BALANCER.

WHEN YOUR SOUL NEEDS ASSISTANCE, REACH
OUT AND ALLOW YOURSELF TO CONNECT WITH
AID. RELIEF IS FOUND IN THE COMFORTS OF
COLLABORATION.

I don't need to know you to love you.

I'M PROUD OF YOU.
I GIVE YOU PERMISSION TO FEED YOUR
POSITIVE SELF-NARRATIVE.

I CAN'T WAIT FOR YOU TO TELL THE STORY THAT
HEALS YOUR WHOLE SELF.

I BELIEVE IN YOU.
YOU ARE SO CAPABLE.

Our story of trust is a pivotal arc in our life story.

WHAT'S YOURS SOUND LIKE?

What trust looks like,
and how our
interpretation of it feels,
is a central part of our
ability to find alignment
within ourselves, in the
now.

Self-trust is the
foundation for all trust,
because it's where the
story of confidence
comes to life, in every
situation, every day.

Being alive means experiencing movement in many directions.

SOMETIMES, EVERYTHING IS EXPERIENCED AS BEING IN BALANCED HARMONY, AND OTHER TIMES, THERE MAY BE SEVERAL THREADS SEVERELY OUT OF WHACK.

ALL IS WELL.
ALL IS AN OPPORTUNITY FOR PROGRESSION.

We learn to trust ourselves by becoming aware, fully embodied, grounded in the moment, and by letting the clarity of quiet stillness resonate through our entire being.

Take it Easy

THE FASTER WE THINK, MOVE, AND DO, THE
LESS WE DISCERN THOUGHTFULLY, MOVE
WISELY, AND DO WHAT IS IN OUR OWN BEST
INTEREST.

This Is It

THE SACRED PAUSE.

LET IT SIT.

DIGEST IT.

SINK INTO THE STILLNESS.

Clear your Channels

WHEN WE CAN RESONATE AS A CLEAR CONDUIT
FOR THE ENERGIES OF LIFE, INSPIRATION
POURS IN EFFORTLESSLY.

ALLOW THE HEART AND MIND TO ABSORB
FLASHES OF BRILLIANCE AND JOY IN A
CONTINUIM OF INPUT AND OUTPUT THAT FLOWS
FREELY WITHOUT THE DISRUPTION OF FORCE OR
ATTACHMENT.

Quiet Down.

BE SETTLED. ALLOW THE QUIET TO COMPLIMENT
THE SOUND.

Balance sways.

Balance is an active process; whether you are standing on your head, or wading through the issues in your mind or heart.

Scout the Non-ordinary

MAKE TIME TO LET GO OF YOUR AUTOMATIC
YANG BEHAVIORS NOW AND THEN. SINK INTO
RIGHT NOW INSTEAD. FEEL WHERE YOU ARE
TODAY, NOTICE YOUR EDGES. ALLOW YOUR BODY
TO INVITE YOU DEEPER INTO THE SUBTLE
UNDERTONES OF NON-ORDINARY POTENTIAL.

You are the Storyteller
of this Narrative.

MAY YOU LET THIS TRUTH BE THE SIGNIFICANT
DIFFERENCE THAT ALLOWS YOU TO TRANSCEND
HOLLOW DRIVES AND FIND THE LIMITLESS
BASIN OF YOUR ENERGETIC, CONFIDENT
MOTIVATION AND CLARITY.

Choose Your Path

THERE ARE SO MANY MORE PATHS TO
DYSFUNCTION THAN TO FUNCTION. NEITHER IS
MORE ACCESSIBLE OR CHALLENGING AT ANY
GIVEN MOMENT, BUT THE CUMULATIVE RESULTS
OF REPEATED DYSFUNCTION STEER YOU
FARTHER AND FARTHER AWAY FROM PURPOSE.

THE GOOD NEWS IS IF YOU CAN LEARN THE
DEEPLY SEATED LESSONS FOUND IN THE
DYSFUNCTION, FUNCTIONAL CHOICES RING SO
TRUE TO YOUR HEART THAT IN TIME, THEY
BECOME THE EASILY PREFERRED CHOICE.

Select Your Narrative

WHETHER IT'S GROWTH, HEALING, OR
ABUNDANCE THAT YOU SEEK, YOUR NARRATIVE
SETS THE TONE AND STEERS EVERYTHING ELSE
INTO BEING, OR OBLITERATION.

RIGHT HERE, RIGHT NOW, CAN YOU SEE WHERE
REGENERATION IS TAKING PLACE IN YOU AND
YOUR LIFE?

Without Stipulation

LOVE BIG.

LEARN TO LOVE THE WORLD,
AND YOURSELF,
IN THEIR ENTIRETY,

THERE IS
SOPHISTICATION IN

Noticing

Sophistication in Noticing

Noticing is one of the essential steps of connection to yourself and everything else. It's easier to walk around like a horse wearing blinders, and while some functions and tasks require that, in brevity, we miss opportunities to notice things all the time.

Think of when someone noticed a detail that you appreciated, but wouldn't have been able to tap into if somebody hadn't blatantly pointed out? How do you take that appreciation and turn it into a commitment to become the noticer?

Ego, Body, Spirit, and Space - A tall tale

The Ego, the Body, and the Spirit all wanted to live a human life, and of these three, only Spirit had the celestial means to make it happen.

"Use my limbs and my senses, great Spirit! I will concede all directions if you can breathe life into my form," the Body cried, for he was listless and dull without animation.

"Give me means, and I shall make the experience great, and prove our amalgamation important!" cried the Ego, for, without the others, he also was listless and would forever remain unseen.

"I shall take us on a grand adventure my loves and fused, each with our functional purpose, we will complete a mission, navigated terrestrially in human form," the Spirit consented.

As he fused the two and stood before them at his feet, he explained several pivotal caveats.

"You must understand, without my presence, we have no essence to keep us formed or the ability to soak up the meaning in the adventure. You must always let me lead, for the senses that Body brings are but tendrils to soak up the information we must sort. While the will and drive of Ego are pivotal to the shape of our intellect, movement, and function, only I can animate us as one, decipher the journey, and lead us safely home again."

Without another murmur, Spirit stepped inside, created the human vessel they should wield in unison.

The Body, infused with consciousness, heard the words of Spirit but immediately became absorbed by touch, tastes, sights, smells and sounds that shrouded him.

The Ego, permeated by thought, will, and deep cognition, heard the whisper but busily preoccupied himself in devising plans, ideas, and dreams, compulsively stretching the new limbs and senses at his disposal.

Pausing in the suit, Spirit settled in, observing quietly as the Body absorbed itself wherever and with whatever the Ego dragged it and demanded. Spirit witnessed in silence how Ego celebrated dominion over Body without consideration and flitted about using him to affect the physical world in pursuit of his passions and flights of fancy. Snuggled deep within and letting the other two manifest as they wished without argument, Spirit got nice and cozy, remaining unattached to the intricacies of the journey's steerage, consigned to do his intrinsic job.

From that comfy space, he traveled, smiling reflectively at himself, "When they figure it out, I will be here, full of all the knowledge and noticing that they dismissed along the way. From the beginning, I had every answer that they seek, every validation that they crave, and every wisdom that continues to elude them."

Every day and every night, Spirit watched on with love and prayer for his companions;

"Sweet Body, may you be happy for the charged relay of your senses that come and go until you've had your fill and can die and be re-birthed of the elements again. Hasty though you begin, you will discover that each sensory perception is no better or worst than the last. All are fleeting and worthy of honor."

"Dear Ego, may you find peace in the eventual revelation that your feelings and affectations of worldly importance are, but extensions of your imagination; your best work was that which you busily discarded and assumed meant nothing. By the end of this journey, you will look back forlorn, for everything that you focused on intently meant far less than the fact that you are a sheer miracle of existence."

"Sometimes we can only find our true direction when we let the wind of change carry us."

- Mimi Novic

Is There Meaning in This?

CONSIDER WHATEVER COMES TO MIND.
DO WE INVENT THE MEANING OR IS IT INNATE?

Being alive means experiencing movement in many directions.

SOMETIMES, EVERYTHING IS EXPERIENCED AS
BEING IN BALANCED HARMONY,
AND OTHER TIMES, THERE MAY BE SEVERAL
THREADS SEVERELY OUT OF WHACK.

ALL IS WELL.
ALL IS AN OPPORTUNITY FOR PROGRESSION.

Where do you turn when you're looking for peace?

IS IT TIME TO LIGHTEN YOUR LOAD?

SET DOWN YOUR BAGGAGE; IT NEED NOT
MIGRATE WITH US FROM HERE. AS THE DAY
FADES INTO HISTORY, WE CONSCIOUSLY
CHOOSE TO STEP INTO THE NEW YEAR WITH
INTENTION, HOPE, AND GRATITUDE. FREED OF
ALL THE YEARS AND THINGS THAT CAME
BEFORE, WE ALLOW OUR VISION TO CLEAR. OUR
HEARTS OPEN, AND OUR MINDS INFUSED WITH
ALL THE POTENTIAL BRIMMING FROM WITHIN.

FULL or empty?

The pendulum swings and vascillates.

THERE IS NO PROBLEM WITH EITHER STATE. IT
JUST IS WHAT IT IS, WHEN IT IS. PAY
ATTENTION TO WHEN YOUR ENERGY IS RUNNING
ON EMPTY AND TAKE THE TIME THAT IT TAKES
TO REFILL AND RE-NOURISH YOURSELF.

REFRAME
Full

"FULL IS GOOD" ISN'T AN ABSOLUTE.
WHEN THE MIND STAYS FULL ALL THE TIME,
THERE IS NO REAL SPACE FOR BEING.
INSTEAD OF STRIVING TO BE EVER-FULL, TRY
ACCEPTING NATURAL FLUX AND VARIATION.

CREATE SPACE FOR TRANSIENT FULLNESS.
GIVE AND TAKE IN BALANCE.

Reset the Clock

DO YOU WATCH THE CLOCK, ALWAYS
ANTICIPATING, OR DO YOU TRANSCEND TIME BY
BEING FULLY IN EACH MOMENT? THE THING
ABOUT THE LIFE THAT WE ARE LIVING IN IS,
TIME IS A MANUFACTURED UNIT OF MEASURE.
THE EXPERIENCE OF EACH MOMENT IS ALL THAT
WE HAVE.

IRONICALLY, TIME AND MONEY ARE VERY
SIMILAR; WE FIND IT EASIER TO BELIEVE THAT
WE DON'T HAVE ENOUGH OF EITHER. THE TRUTH
IS, WE HAVE EXACTLY WHAT WE NEED RIGHT
NOW. CAN WE LEARN TO ALLOW THAT TO BE
ENOUGH?

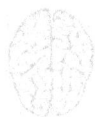

When we're thriving, positivity and perspective take center stage.

IT DOESN'T MEAN THAT WE DON'T ENCOUNTER
OBSTACLES OR HAVE TO WORK HARD. IT JUST
MEANS THAT WE'RE CONNECTED, JOYFUL, AND
MAKING PROGRESS IN A STATE OF GRATITUDE.

TO THRIVE

We must make mindfully calculated adjustments.

AS OUR LIVES, THOUGHTS, AND BEHAVIORS
WERE FORMED BY US, THEY CAN BE REFORMED
AND TRANSFORMED BY US AS WELL.

REBUILD WHAT CALLS FOR UPDATING.
LET IT RING TRUER TO WHO YOU ARE.

FINE-TUNE WHAT'S RIGHT.
KICK EVERYTHING LESS THAN DESIRABLE THAN
THAT TO THE CURB.

Healing

IF NOTHING EVER CHANGES, CAN YOU DIG DEEP
WITHIN AND FIND THE STRENGTH TO FEEL
WHOLE IN SPITE OR IT?

REHABILITATION BEGINS IN THE HEARTS OF
EACH INDIVIDUAL. TO RECONCILE OUR
SUFFERING, WE ASK OUR HEARTS TO ADOPT THE
GRACE OF ACCEPTANCE.

Peace

WHY ARE WE SO QUICK TO FEED ANGER WHEN
PEACE IS THE MORE NATURAL STATE?

HOLDING ON TO ANGER TAKES SO MUCH MORE
ENERGY THAN LETTING IT GO.

HOW CAN YOU DISCHARGE THIS EXCESS
NEGATIVITY MORE REGULARLY? HOW CAN YOU
CLEAN UP THE IMPACT OF STOWED AWAY ANGER
AND RELEASE IT TO CREATE MORE PEACE
WITHIN?

PEACE INSIDE = PEACE IN YOUR LIFE

Observe.

Align.

Repeat.

SOMETIMES YOU WILL LISTEN TO, AND BELIEVE
IN, THE PEOPLE AND THINGS THAT ARE WRONG
FOR YOU. THERE IS A TRANSFORMATIVE
FUNCTION IN THIS.

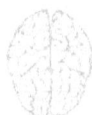

You're Not Stuck

IT IS POSSIBLE YOU'RE A BIT DISCONNECTED.

LET GO OF ACCUMULATED DEFENSES.
GET GROUNDED.
CENTERED.
CALM.

EVEN THE BITE OF LOVE LOST, SINGED, OR
STUNG HOLDS LESSONS AND
OPPORTUNITIES.LOVE IS A NATURAL WAY.

OPEN UP AND INVITE IT IN.

MARINATE IN YOUR DEVOTION.

BE STEERED BY THE FLOW OF LOVE'S
RESOUNDING MESSAGES, AND NEVER CEASE TO
LET LOVE RADIATE TOO AND FROM YOU.

REOPEN THE GATES.

Step Outside of Batiles

PUT DOWN THE ARROWS.
WE NEEDN'T PIERCE OR HARM ANOTHER,
OR OURSELVES.

AS WE SET OUR ARROWS TO REST,
WE TOO ARE STRAIGHTED OUT,
RESTORED TO ALIGNMENT.

ONLY FROM HERE CAN WE FIND THE STRENGTH
TO FLY EXPERTLY UPON THE WIND.

Act it Out

DO SOMETHING ABOUT YOUR PROBLEMS.

PRAY, MEDITATE, AND ACT ON SOLUTIONS TO
REMEDY WHAT AILS YOU.

IT'S NOT ABOUT WHAT YOU DO;
IT'S ABOUT HOW YOU DO IT,
AND THAT YOU TAKE THE TIME THAT IT TAKES
TO DO IT.

EMPHASIS LINGERS ON THE "DOING."

Self-Compassion starts
with noticing what you
need, by taking step back
from the tunnel vision of
what you want.

FROM THE DEPTHS OF YOUR BEING, WHAT DO
YOU TRULY NEED TODAY?

How does trusting myself influence my relationships?

CAN TRUSTING MYSELF FULLY MAKE IT EASIER
TO ACCEPT ALL TYPES OF CHANGE?

Pick One:

Restrictive

Retaliatory

Resilient

*WHICH RESPONSE ARE YOU MOST PARTIAL TO?

IS THAT THE REACTION TO LIFE THAT YOU MOST
WANT TO STRNGTHEN?

THERE IS WISDOM IN

Nature

Natural Wisdoms

'Natural' is a word that we use to describe the existence of the collective phenomenon around us. In nature, we observe simple things such as how a tree does not try to be a river, nor the sun strives to be like the moon. Without trying to be anything, they are each what they are, and they are whole. In their native states, they embrace the essence of what is and live out their experiences from that vantage point.

What separates humans from this natural state is their ability to ignore, deny, and reject it. Either way, it's up to you.

All of nature exists in a state of chaos that manifests as cycles, equilibrium, and compatibility. In a sense, it is a systematic organic unfolding. In nature, we are what we are, as we are, how we are, and that's okay.

Our experience of nature is painted through the lens of our worldview. Life is energy. Within the synergy of life and death is a beautiful cyclical and ceaseless transformation.

"Technology, mechanics, and logic all have their place. They also, however, have their limitations."

- Anne Wilson Shaef

From thoughts and emotions to grand external gestures, we are all experiencing unnoticed movement of many kinds.

AS LONG AS YOU'RE ALIVE, LIFE WILL KEEP HAPPENING TO YOU, FOR YOU, IN YOU, AND ALL AROUND YOU. SWAY IN THE FLOW OF YOUR LIFE'S TAPESTRY.

MAKE MEMORIES

OFT FORGOTTEN ARE THE SIMPLE THINGS.
THE SMALLEST STUFF WHICH MAKES LIFE
WORTH LIVING.

THE SONGS OF THE BIRD,
THE AROMA OF COOKING,
SMILES THAT RESONATE FROM GUT TO EYES.

Be Friendly With All

MAKE FRIENDS OF ALL KINDS.
LET THEM STRENGTHEN YOUR LOVE.
PEACE IS MAKING HONEST CONNECTIONS.

GREAT JOY RESIDES WITHIN YOU.
SHARE THAT WITH COURAGE.

THIS IS EXISTENCE

LEARN TO BE HERE FULLY.

EXIST LOVINGLY, THOUGHTFULLY,
AND WITH INNATE GRATITUDE.

WE MUSTN'T RUSH THE MIRACLE TO FRUITION.

ALL WILL TRANSPIRE IN INTUITIVE TIME.

REJOICE IN THE ABUNDANCE OF LIFE AS IT
APPEARS IN THE NOW.

AFTER ALL, YOU, TOO,
ARE A BLOSSOM OF DIVINE LOVE.

Perfection is a False Belief

TOTAL CONTROL IS AN ILLUSION.

Let experiences unfold to you
through the perception of
imperfections,

Knowing it is the loving sway of
the whole.

Balance cloaks itself in chaos.
This is simply nature's way.

Embrace Your Companions

MAY EVERY ACQUAINTANCE AND
COMPANION ARISE TO YOU WITH LOYAL
PROTECTION.ALL SEPARATE, AND YET
INTERCONNECTED; ACKNOWLEDGE THE
BIGGER SCHEME OF EVERY FOE AND ALLY.

There are no exclusions
in the family of being

WE CAN HONOR EACH COMPANIONS
IN ADMIRATION OF THEIR PLACE, IN THIS SPACE,
FOR THIS TIME. FRET NOT OVER THE THREADED
JOURNEY OF ANOTHER.

APPRECIATE
The Creatures

YOU TOO ARE ONE.

THE TAME AND THE WILD ARE ALL AT HOME
HERE.

TOGETHER, IN HARMONY, WE EXIST.

BIG OR SMALL IN STATURE, WE ALL PLAY A
PART IN THE STORY THAT IS LIFE.

ONE IS NOT AVAILABLE WITHOUT THE OTHER.

THE FABRIC OF LIFE MUST BE WOVEN WITH
CARE, AWARENESS, AND SUBTLETY.

PREPARE IT ALWAYS TO STRETCH AND BEND
WITHOUT DAMAGE.

Let Nature lead.
In nature, there is
always an inherent
flow.Take a breath and
rejoin with yours.Trek
back to the current,
which instinctively
pulsates your essence
outward.

Bend and Sway with Changes.

THIS IS A JOURNEY OF MOVEMENT, EVEN IN THE
STILLNESS.

Ground into the Earth
that you Grace. Like the
tree, stand tall and still,
day and night, breathing
in deeply the sweet
elixirs of life.

LET YOUR ROOTS PRELUDE ONLY THE BRANCHES
THAT GIVE YOU ULTIMATE SHAPE. GROW INTO
YOUR NATURAL STATE OF BEING;
INDIVIDUALIZED BUT NOT SEPARATED. MAY
YOUR LEAVES BE BOUNTIFUL IN
CHARACTER, PLENTIFUL IN EXPRESSION, AND
COURAGEOUSLY UNFOLDING INTO THE LIGHT.

Explore
The Human Forest

A FOREST IS MADE OF MANY TREES.

HONOR THE BEAUTY OF ITS
INDIVIDUALS, WITHOUT DISCARDING THEIR SUM
INTELLIGENCE.

LET EACH TREE BE AS YOU ARE;
RISING FROM A SPECIFIC SET OF ROOTS,
GROWING LIMBS IN RESPONSE TO ELEMENTS,
AND FLOWERING IN MANY COLORS AS YOU ARCH
YOURSELF FORWARD UNTO THE SUN.

SPROUT UP
& Spring Forth

FROM THE ROOTS AND UPWARD, YOU GROW
TALLER, MORE DURABLE, WISER. SUMMON
ALWAYS YOUR STRENGTH FROM THE DEEP AND
RADIATE TOWARD THE SKY. IN HARMONY, WALK
THE SHOULD AND COULD OF HUMAN LIFE ON A
SACRED PATH.

The World Is A Mirror

LIFE UNIFIES US WITH WHAT WE ALREADY
KNOW.

IT IS THE SHRINE WITHIN, THAT HOLDS THE
TREASURES, THAT SPEAK THE LANGUAGE OF
OUR HEARTS.

THIS SOUND IS THE INTONATION OF OUR
HARMONY OR DISPARITY WITH THE WORLD.

IN SILENCE, WE FIND A PASSAGE TO THE
INTERIOR SPRINGS, THAT SHAPE OUR
TONALITIES.

Are you in season?

SELF SHIFTS IN EVERY SEASON.

EVERY DISCOVERY AT THE ALTAR OF SELF
SHAPES A NEW MELODIC MODULATION.

THERE, IN THE QUIET, WE BEGIN TO
CONSOLIDATE OUR TRUE KNOWING.

COLLECTIVELY, HUMANITY IS OUR
FOREST, UNVEILING WONDROUS VARIETIES OF
WISDOM TO PLAY WITH, FOR AND AGAINST OUR
INTERIOR CHORDS.

Stand In Awe

IN AWE OF A LANDSCAPE.
AMAZED BY YOUR COMPANIONS.
SETTLED IN TO THE COMFORT OF HOME;
THESE ARE THE RHYTHMS OF LOVE.
IN YOUR ESSENCE YOU CARRY THEM ALL.
CARRY THEM TENDERLY, ALL OF YOUR DAYS.
TO EVERY SPACE AND PLACE YOU TREK,
RECEIVE THEM WITH GRATITUDE.

GRATITUDE RECIPROCATES AWE.
THESE ARE YOUR BIGGEST BLESSINGS.

Divine Connectivity

JUST AS WE ARE WOVEN INTO THE INTRICATE
FABRIC OF LIFE, ALL OTHER BEINGS ARE ALSO
THREADED THROUGH WITH DIVINE
CONNECTIVITY.

THE UNIVERSAL LOOM WEAVES MINDFULLY, IN
INFINITE UNITY, AND YOU ARE A PART OF THAT
DIVINE PLAN.

REGARD OTHERS WITH THE SAME RESPECT YOU
CONSTRUCT TOWARDS SELF.

WE ARE ALL WORTHY OF THE SAFETY AND
APPRECIATION THAT WE SEEK.

THERE IS RELIEF IN

Allowing

Relief Through Allowing

The only way to eradicate all the exaggerated doubt that we carry is to rewrite our conditioned mental chatter script and relearn how to take action with faith. Don't delay overcoming your challenges simply because a little fear accompanies change. In allowing, we make room for renewal. Allow without resistance. Allowing is a path to removing internal blocks and connected instead with the loving essence of spirit. To be rich with purpose is to move with greater abundance and connection in all that you do.

We all arrive at crossroads where we realize that we've gotten stuck in old stories. Transitions aren't always easy. As you come to this latest juncture of change, I know that it's a beautiful gift to be capable of cleaning your internal house again.

Pave the way for a new narrative. In asking ourselves, "How can I be of Help or service?" We balance the ego's journey of self-entitlement. If we and everyone we know could migrate to this way of thinking in tandem, how fewer messes we'd all find ourselves in. When you learn to listen closely to the stresses of self and others, solutions frequently become clear.

Communities that work together experience far less strife than those steeped in a mass sense of the individual self-entitlement. To be of service is to heal yourself and all of your surroundings.

Take the time that it takes to reflect upon the flow of the sacred stream.
Surrender yourself to its wisdom.
Intuitively, be pulled only towards that which grows, flows, and edges the journey forward.
Surrender to where the flow takes you.

Let go of everything no longer serving you. Progress with the stream.

The only way to eradicate doubt is to take action with faith. Don't delay overcoming your challenges simply because a little fear accompanies change. In allowing, we make room for renewal. Allow without resistance. This is a path to removing internal blocks and connected instead with the loving essence of spirit. To be rich with purpose is to move with greater abundance and connection in all that you do.

"Getting over a painful experience is much like crossing monkey bars. You have to let go at some point in order to move forward."
- C.S. Lewis

Not every path will be linear.

YOUR CURRENT LATITUDE IS A
MATTER OF PERCEPTION.
IMAGINE YOUR JOURNEY BEYOND
LINEAR TIMELINES AND BOSES.
SURRENDER TO THE WONDROUS
FLUX OF GROWTH AND SENSATIO.

I grant myself
the authority to
hold honest
jurisdiction over
my life.

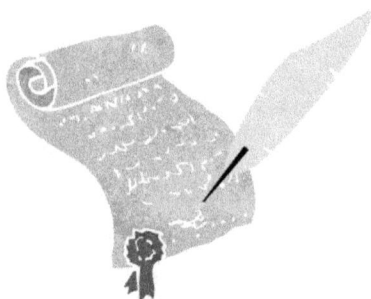

You are Complete.

THE SEARCH FOR WHOLENESS
IS A HANDY ROUTE,
BUT NEVER, NOT EVEN FOR A MOMENT, ARE YOU
INCOMPLETE.

ADOPT LAYERS OF PERSPECTIVE TO NOURISH
THE SPAN OF YOUR VOYAGE.

WHETHER YOUR SHIFTING BETWEEN LAYERS OR
DANCING AMID POLARITIES, YOUR MINDSET
DIVINES YOUR EXPERIENCE.

CONSTRUCT AN ATTITUDE OF
OBJECTIVITY, ONE THAT STRETCHES ACROSS
THE MENAGERIE WITH ADMIRATION.

Befriend the MindBody, Beautiful.

WHEN WE CONDITION OURSELVES TO ATTEND
AND BEFRIEND OURSELVES FIRST,
WE SET THE STAGE FOR THE MOST MARVELOUS
THINGS TO HAPPEN.

YOU ARE AN EMBODIMENT OF POISE.

HOW CAN YOU LIVE FROM THAT GROUNDED
PLATFORM OF COMPOSURE TODAY?

For today,
and in the days ahead,
may you become fully
conscious that every
moment has its time.

If 'Tis not here now, it simply does not belong to this day, and that's okay.

Intuit

THINK ABSTRACTLY.

ACT WITH LOVE.

CONNECT WITH COMPASSION,
AND SING THE MESSAGES OF YOUR HEART.

YOUR PURPOSE MAY NEVER BE FULLY KNOWN TO
YOU,

AND THAT IS A BEAUTIFUL THING.

EVERY DAY, YOU HOLD THE AMPLITUDE OF
MIRACLE, CATALYST, AND MUSE.

MIRACLES

ACKNOWLEDGE THE ELEMENTAL MIRACLES.

LIFE IS A MIRACLE
OF MANY ESSENTIAL ELEMENTS,
ALL WORKING IN SEAMLESS COLLABORATION
FOR THE WHOLE TO THRIVE.

SIMPLY ALLOW THIS TO BE SO.
MORE IS DELIVERED TO THE WILLING
THAN TO THE WILL ALONE.

SEEK ALIGNMENT WITHIN,
IN TANDEM WITH OUTWARD HARMONY.

Allow it

THERE MAY BE DAYS WHEN YOU FEEL HEAVY.

THAT TOO,
YOU MUST LEARN TO DRINK IN & ALLOW.

GREAT SORROW IS A SERRATION FROM THE BIG
JOYS THAT YOU HAVE KNOWN.

HONOR THAT.

TRANSFORMATION IS THE WAY OF NATURE.

FEEL THE WAVES OF ALL EMOTIONS WITH
GRATITUDE.

HONOR THE TIME AND FUNDAMENTAL PURPOSE
OF ALL STATES OF BEING.

DON'T CLING,
EMBRACE AND THEN DISSOLVE.

Nurture the witness.

Nourish your soul.

It is you, and you are she.

Gravitas

THE GRAVITAS OF LOVE IS HEAVY AND DEEP.
FALLING TO EARTH,
TO SPRING TO LIFE,
WE FIND OURSELVES EMBODIED.

FOSTER THIS RICH DEEP LOVE.
CARRY IT WITH YOU.
ALLOW IT TO LIGHTEN YOUR EXPERIENCE.

EMBRACE ITS COLORS.
TASTE OF ITS FLAVORS.
ABOSORB THE TEXTURES IT LENDS TO LIFE.

BE JUST AS YOU ARE.
THE AGING CHILD,
EXACTLY AS YOU WERE INTENDED

Be Rooted

WHEN WE'RE HERE, IN THE NOW,
THERE IS NO NEED FOR EXCUSES OR
ACCOMMODATIONS.

JUST BE.
ROOTED IN SAFETY.
WRAPPED IN LOVE.

Shine

THE LIGHT WITHIN SHINES BRIGHTEST WHEN
PERMITTED TO DO SO.

YOU ARE THE LIGHT, AND THE GRANTER.

OPEN YOUR CONDUIT:
RECIEVE, INTERACT, AND SHINE.

We can't control the Universe, but we can steer our journey in different directions.

EVEN UNDER THE MOST STRINGENT SURVEILLANCE, LIFE QUICKLY UNFOLDS IN UNEXPECTED WAYS.

Trust Your Alignment

CHOOSE TO LIVE IN ALIGNMENT WITH WHAT
LIFE WANTS FOR YOU;

IT IS MORE INCREDIBLE AND VAST THAN YOU
CAN FORCE INTO BEING ON YOUR OWN.

ALIGN AND YOUR DREAMS WILL DIVINE INTO
BEING.

You're unlocking the doors of your spirit, and there is no cause for overwhelm.

GO BACK AT ANY TIME AND NOURISH ALL THE ASPECTS OF SELF THAT YOU MAY HAVE ABSENT-MINDEDLY NEGLECTED.

Today is an opportunity to make incredible discoveries.

INVITE WINDS OF CHANGE FLOW OVER YOU.
OPEN TO THE DESIRES OF YOUR HEART.

Time Turns All Things Into Something New

TIME EVOLVES ALL THINGS.

CONSTELLATIONS SHIFT.

SEASONS PASS.

WATERS PUSH FROM SHORE.

SEE THE WITNESS FOR WHAT SHE IS:
EVER-EVOLVING.

THERE IS CLARITY IN

Questioning

Do you remember when we talked about questioning everything, even if it's just because you can?

Well, here's why. The world today has a lot of 'truths' that get slung around and superimposed onto specific target markets, groups, and communities of all kinds, ALL THE TIME.

I don't have to infuse a sense of challenge into the question, "What if this were it?"Instead, I can consider it for what it is; a simple question.

Can I imagine what total acceptance of "This is it" may look like for me?

Is the truth that I'd be slower, more patient, and way less distractible?

Could I lean into every hug, snuggle, and conversation a little more in-depth?

Would I be more willing to sink into love more fully?

Is it possible to live in a way reflective of the fact that relationships are the most precious, valuable connections in this life?

Is it true that if I accept "this is it," I can let go of selfish impulses and linger a little longer in my appreciation of the world and all of its tiny, precious things instead? Would I be able to embrace better what is right in front of me?

There is no particular belief system that is 'right' or 'wrong.' However, they can sometimes constrain our ability to evolve our truths. As Deborah Adele puts it, *"When we identify with these constraints, we run on old habits, and we consent to be less than we are."* When we allow ourselves to question what we find to be immovable truths, we learn to be pliable in a way that best serves our transitory journey through life.

"The first step towards getting somewhere is to decide you're not going to stay where you are."
—John Pierpont "J.P." Morgan

Is it of value?

IT MATTERS NOT WHERE WE'VE BEEN, BUT HOW
WE'VE ALLOWED IT TO TRANSFORM US FOR THE
BETTER, OR WORSE.

THE PAST IS BUT A TINY PRECURSOR TO THE
VIBRANT STORY LEADING US FORWARD INTO
THE LIGHT.

THE VALUE OF THIS JOURNEY LIVES NOT IN THE
PAST NOR THE FUTURE; THE TREASURE IS ONLY
PRESENT IN THE MOMENT AT HAND.

MINDFULNESS
because 45 times a day,

I GET OVERWHELMED AND HAVE TO ASK
MYSELF, "WHAT AM I DOING?"

- [ ] WHERE ARE YOU?
- [ ] WHAT ARE YOU DOING?
- [ ] WHAT DO YOU NEED?

When we're thrust into something unexpected, suddenly finding ourselves destined for different realities...

WE CAN SLOW DOWN.
WE CAN REMEMBER THAT ALTHOUGH THIS IS
DIFFERENT THAN WE EXPECTED,
ALL IS STILL WELL.

SHIFT GEARS

LIFE SWITCHES TRACKS WITHOUT PRIOR
NOTICE. FOLLOW THE FLOW TO DISCOVER
WHERE YOU'RE BEING LED.

Experiment with every search, standard, and trial.

A TRAIL WITHOUT TRIALS IS A BLAND TASTE OF DESSERT INDEED.

Am I holding on to certain old wounds because I'm so used to the resonant pain & suffering that I find an irrational comfort in the self-torture of continuing to carry them around?

WHAT WEIGHTS AM I ALLOWED TO SHED? HOW WOULD IT FEEL TO SET MYSELF A LITTLE FREER?

Let Your Faith Be Tested

FAITH, LIKE ALL THINGS, SPROUTS, WINDS, WEATHERS, AND GROWS.

THERE IS NO OBSTACLE IT CANNOT PENETRATE.

When in doubt, do not hesitate to reach through the universe.

WISDOM GROWS IN THE SEEKING & DOING.

Travel across the barriers, and down the rabbit holes if you must; Find the truths that you seek.

MAY YOUR GRIT EMBOLDEN YOUR COMPOSURE WITH GRACE.

There are always solutions.

GRATITUDE TO YOUR HUMAN INGENUITY.

What is Constructed Can be Reformed at Any Time.

TIME IS A DISTINCT CONSTRUCT OF THIS JOURNEY.

IT CREATES AND DISMANTLES OUR INTERPRETATIONS OF BEING, WITH DESIGNATIONS OF BEGINNINGS TO END.

MAY YOUR ODYSSEY BE FULL OF COUNTLESSLY VIBRANT DETAILS, TOO TIMELESS TO COMPARTMENTALIZE.

The Journey To Confidence:

IS BUILT UPON THE FOUNDATION OF THINGS WE
DON'T TYPICALLY LIKE. BUT IF THEY BUILD
CONFIDENCE, ARE THEY REALLY BAD AT ALL?

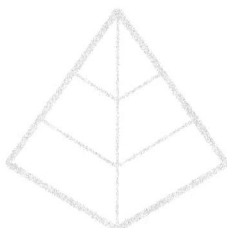

Can you choose love?

THERE IS A CHOICE BETWEEN LOVE OR FEAR.
EVERY DAY, IN EVERY MOMENT, WE MUST
ALWAYS CHOOSE LOVE.

FOR ALL THE THINGS BEYOND OUR CONTROL,
WE GRANT OURSELVES PEACE OF MIND WHEN
WE MUSTER THE COURAGE TO TRUST IN DIVINE
PLANNING FAITHFULLY.

Reframe it

NOTHING STAYS THE SAME.

EVEN DEVASTATING MOMENTS HAVE A WAY OF
STRENGTHENING BONDS.

IN THE SPIRIT OF COMMUNITY, ASSIST IN
REORGANIZING THE GROUP FOR RESILIENCE.

IS IT AS BAD AS YOU INITIALLY THOUGHT,
OR IS IT FODDER FOR INSPIRATION?

Make Trades

DISCARD JUDGMENT
TO MAKE ROOM FOR INTUITION.

MASSAGE YOUR PERSPECTIVE
AND RELAX INTO GROWTH.

RELEASE INTO PEACE,
TAKING WITH YOU ALL YOUR DESPAIR.

IT IS OKAY TO ACCEPT LOVE,
TO EXUDE LOVE,
AND TO CARRY IT WITH YOU.

FREE UP SPACE.
MAKE MEANINGFUL TRADES.
SOFTEN AND BE LOVE.

Empathy
is the balancer of
Shame.

CAN WE INVITE INTO OURSELVES ENOUGH
EMPATHY TO NEUTRALIZE ALL THE IMBALANCES
THAT SHAME HAS DECEIVED US IN TO
BELIEVING?

Study Your Static Cling

WE REPEAT SCENARIOS AND SITUATIONS THAT
HARKEN HARD LESSONS FORTH, AGAIN AND
AGAIN, UNTIL WE FULLY ACCEPT THAT WHICH IS
FOR US AND THAT WHICH IS NOT.

TO DISPEL THE STATIC, YOU MUST SOFTEN
YOUR CLINGING TO THAT WHICH WAS NOT
MEANT FOR YOU, AND LET IT GO.

Consider the Costs of Comfort

THERE IS NO SHAME
IN TAKING PLEASURE IN COMFORT.

AND YET,
NO SITUATION OF COMFORT,
IS WORTH SACRIFICING YOUR INTEGRITY.

FOLLOW YOUR INTEGRITY,
NO MATTER THE COST.

IF IT ISN'T GOOD FOR YOU,
IT WASN'T MEANT FOR YOU.

What Doesn't Serve You?

CAN YOU TRADE IT FOR SOMETHING BETTER?

EXAMPLE:

"JEALOUSY WON'T ELEVATE YOU"

BE INSPIRED INSTEAD OF COMPETITIVE

To Commit or Abandon?

Accept Your Lessons

REST ASSURED THAT THEY ARE AN AMBIVALENT
PREREQUISITE THAT SERVICE THE
DELIVERANCE OF YOUR DESTINY.

WITHOUT WORRY, STEP FULLY INTO
BEING. LISTEN CAREFULLY TO THE SONGS OF
YOUR SOUL. NATURAL IS CONTINUALLY PROVING
THAT IN EACH DAY THAT WE WAKE, WE ARE
BLESSED.

Don't Talk the Talk

IF YOU'RE UNWILLING TO WALK THE WALK.

WHAT DO YOU TALK?
WHAT DO YOU WALK?

THERE IS PROSPERITY IN

Community

Community

This human life on Earth is comprised of a matrix of communities; the natural environment, plants, animals, and of course, other people. From the resonant vibration of who we are as individuals, we exist as a self that frequently interacts with family, friends, and communities on both the local and global scales.

When it comes to relationships, the same rule of resonance applies; we serve ourselves best to harmonize with the collective vibrations.

Relationships within every type of community are essential, changing, and frequently cyclical. You have the calm, centered discernment to identify what does and does not resonate with you, for right now. As much as we have all loved the idea of permanence at one time or another, there is a time, space, and majestic beauty of the existence and cycling of relationships in our lives.

Let What Fits Come and Go

When it is time, letting go of people is an opportunity for release. Once you realize that it's time for that, nothing beneficial is born of avoiding it. It stings when we cling.

We don't have access to the cosmic clock, so whatever the rhyme, reason, or season for shifts in your community, meet the transitions with grace.

This life, and the time that you're gifted to live it, is a miracle. We can't keep others from coming or going as they choose, or as life chooses for them.

They're on their journey, and honestly, we serve ourselves best by staying focused on ours. To collaborate in the community is incredible, but we must allow that to cycle too as we evolve and transform. It's for others, and it's for us.

Whenever necessary, feel your hurts, heal your wounds, and move forward with all the lessons learned and love received under your belt.

This is how we honor ourselves, in honor of all the lovely people that sway in and out, and sometimes through our paths.

It's okay to let the old things go without harboring feelings of hostility, fear, or retaliation to be who you are now. Let them go with great love & empathy, even if you cannot fully comprehend their choices. Seek the communities that soothe where you're at. That's an honor.

Embrace your communities, love them, lend them your brilliance, and collaborate wherever you can. When it's time, for any reason, be prepared to step away with grace. All things change, and in moving on, we're creating space for a different community that needs us.

In our commitment to naturally resonate, we never default on our integrity by acting impulsively out of character. We are in tune.

Though the facets, labels, and characters we create may vary, we are all made of the same interior fabric of the soul.

Each of us is still learning to relate to the world through these bodies. Through this flesh, we connect to society.

Let your stories be written, with only the ethos of your transformative essence at their core.

It's okay to be alone.

AS PART OF OUR INTERIOR BALANCE,
THE ABILITY TO BE PEACEFUL AND FULFILLED
IN OUR OWN COMPANY IS A GIFT.

IN THIS SPACE, WE FILL OURSELVES UP AGAIN,
TAKING THE TIME THAT IT TAKES TO BE OUR
OWN INDIVIDUAL, JUST AS WE ARE, WITHOUT
THE INFLUENCE OF OTHERS.

HERE IS WHERE WE SORT THROUGH OUR OWN
STUFF WITH CURIOSITY AND SELF-COMPASSION.

WHEN IT IS TIME TO RE-EMERGE, WE ARE
FORTIFIED TO DANCE IN BALANCE WITH
COMMUNITY AGAIN.

Today, find the quiet
stillness of a single
moment, and remember
how to trust yourself
completely.

WHAT DOES THAT LOOK LIKE?
HOW DOES IT FEEL?

FIND YOUR RHYTHM

EMBRACE THE RHYTHMS THAT USHER YOU
FORWARD.

BE EVER CURIOUS, WALKING DIRECTLY TO
WHERE YOU ARE MOST CALLED.

REMEMBER MY LOVE, THAT INTENTION
MANIFESTS DELIGHT.

UNDERSTAND THAT EVERY ENCHANTMENT IS A
COMPANION OF SORROW IN SOME WAY.

TRANSITIONS ARE THE ACCORD OF LIVING
CONSCIOUSNESS.

CONNECTED.FLOWING.LAYERED.

Within the sacred pact of trusting ourselves, we learn to connect with others without the distortion of our projections.

What types of
communities suit
your soul?

What shared
values are they
built upon?

We know it doesn't feel good when relationship boundaries migrate, but just as we are hardwired to prefer what we know, it doesn't mean that it's a bad thing.

HOW HAVE YOU BEEN EVOLVING?

Boundaries are always migratory.

NOTHING IS FIXED, EXCEPT MAYBE OUR EGO
EXPECTATIONS THAT IT SHOULD BE.

To be let down, or to let others down, is to excavate the natural discrepancies of how our unspoken expectations land in the world.

WITHOUT A LITTLE RUB, THERE IS NO SHINE.

Levied against the views and expectations of others, our inner truths spark the minor chaos that birth our deepened clarity.

HOW CAN I HONOR CHANGES THAT SUPPORT MY DEEPENING CLARITY?

Trust does fall
And at times we weep
But in wisdom grow
And reground our seat.
Centered in truth,
There is a way to find
Trust restored and truth to bind.

Trust in relationships is a contract of faith with another human being.

NOT ALL CONTRACTS ARE UPHELD.
IT'S OKAY TO EXPERIENCE BREACHES WITHOUT
SHAME OR BLAME.

LET IT FEEL THE WAY IT FEELS.
THEN LET IT GO.

The levels of trust that we choose to extend outward are determined by the boundaries and expectations that we extend with them.

WE DECIDE WHAT TO EXTEND, AND BY DEFINITION, ACCEPT THAT WE HAVE NO CONTROL OVER HOW IT IS TREATED ONCE RECEIVED. WE HOPE, SURE, BUT THERE IS NO GUARANTEE, WHICH IS IN ESSENCE WHAT MAKES TRUST FEEL SO SACROSANCT.

Can I let go of my false sense of control long enough to ask meaningful questions?

HOW WOULD WE EVER WADE PASSED THE MUNDANE WORLD TO UNCOVER THE PATH TO OUR TRUTH IF OUR CURRENT IDEAS WERE NEVER SHATTERED?

In a world of 7.7 billion people:

LONELINESS CAN ONLY AFFECT US WHEN WE WILLINGLY BECKON IT FORWARD AND ELECT TO REINFORCE IT.

Our Loneliness is a product

OF OUR OWN SYSTEMATIC WITHDRAWAL FROM
THE COMMUNITY THAT SURROUNDS US.

Find Your People

IF YOU HAVEN'T FOUND THEM YET.

OUT THERE, SOMEHWERE, THERE'S A TRIBE
WAITING FOR YOU TO COME HOME.

Love is the beacon light of any place that we call home.

UNDERSTANDING IS THE BEAT OF A TRIBE.

IN COOPERATION, THE HEART ALWAYS FINDS A WAY. EVEN IF EVERYTHING ELSE SHOULD FALL TO RUIN, LET LOVE WARM YOU IN ITS SWEET EMBRACE.

BE HELD, WRAPPED IN ARMS OF SAFETY AND COMPASSION.

THERE IS FREEDOM IN

Knowing

Lean in to Knowing

As we attune to who we are and embrace it, we circulate and exist with easier access to higher insight levels. We trust ourselves and gain the confidence to respond to life instead of merely reacting to it.

With slow, deliberate practice, we synergistically elevate our inner knowing and simultaneously raise our vibration. The impact of this is like ripples of positivity set out into the stream of the collective pulses that surround us.

By tuning into self, we can choose to suffer nothing today. Tapping into that guidance and honoring it through action allows us to reach across all layers of confusion until only truth resounds. Centered in the connection of our inner knowing, we nourish self with all that is needed. Grounding into the day with gratitude and courage, you get to choose to live in the ways that matter the most to you, and to serve your community in the ways that support them, and you, best.

Walk Your Talk

Breathe.

Find your center and cozy up into it.

Release the emotional energy flitting around in your chest.

Let go of the thoughts grinding in your mind.

Focus only on your breath.

Within all the life-giving depths and textures of our breath, we learn to create space and embody calm. Here, we tap into divine guidance, and here, we allow it to share, calm and guide our every way. Play with your breath, dance with it, and know that you are the gateway to your every reality. Mindful of your breath, walk your talk and allow it to unfold you, never hijacked by the faulty promises of an ego will. Take the time to your work, the real work that connects you to this life. Practice the walk and let your breath sustain you.

Activate the Mind's Eye

BE WILLING TO SEE THROUGH MIRRORS,
PRISMS, AND PARADIGMS.

EVERY DAY, WE EACH MODEL, MOLD, AND
INVENT OURSELVES THROUGH THE STORIES
THAT WE INSERT TO MIND.

MINDFULLY OBSERVE, AND CURATE YOUR STORY
WITH KINDNESS.

Self-Care requires saying "YES" to You.

NOURISHING YOURSELF, ON A ROUTINE BASIS, BREATHES HEALTHY BOUNDARIES INTO YOUR LIFE.

You Know This

YOU HAVE ALWAYS BEEN LOVED AND LOVEABLE.

Be Spacious

EXPRESS WISDOM AND FORGIVENESS FREELY.

LIFE IS A JOURNEY OF MOVING ON.

TRAVEL IN THE FREEDOM OF NOW.

IN UNION IS THE ONLY WAY TO LOVE.

LOVE IS THE BINDER OF ALL THINGS.

Show up.

WHEN ALL ELSE FAILS, JUST SHOW UP.

SHOW UP FOR YOURSELF IN EVERY MOMENT.

KEEP COMING BACK TO THE MESSAGES OF HOPE
THAT REFRESH YOU, TO THE CIRCLES OF
SUPPORT THAT NURTURE YOU, TO THE TRUTH
THAT YOU ARE CAPABLE.

KEEP COMING BACK TO CENTER.

Be At Ease.

YOU ARE AS YOU ARE.
THERE IS UNQUANTIFIABLE BEAUTY IN THAT.

LET GO OF YOUR STRUGGLES WITH THE PAST,
AND SETTLE INTO THE CLARITY.

SERENITY IS AVAILABLE AT ALL TIMES.

EASE INTO HEALING.

LET YOUR LIFE BE A TESTAMENT TO THE CLEAR
CHOICES OF THIS MOMENT.

EVERY CHOICE IS A CHANCE TO MAKE A
PIVOTAL CHANGE.

Make Your Mark

BE COURAGEOUS. BE BRAVE.
LET YOUR MARK CAUSE NO PAIN TO OTHERS.

HEED LOVINGLY A CALL FOR HEALING WOUNDS,
NOT CREATING THEM.

You are pivotal without
trying to be so. Take
heed of this for when
one works too
hard, there is pain where
only surrender needed
to dwell.

Kindly

BE BOLD AND BRILLIANT.
BE WHATEVER IT IS THAT YOU DESIRE.
ABOVE ALL THOUGH, BE LOVE.

KINDNESS IS LOVE.
WITH UNSHAKEABLE FAITH,
PEACE DELIVERS YOU
WHERE YOU MOST WANT TO GO.

FLOW EVERLASTING TO THE FREEDOMS FOUND
WITHIN THIS LIFE AND LOOK FORWARD TO THE
GIFTS BEYOND YOUR PHYSICAL INCARNATION.

Full Circle,
No Real Repeats

REPETITIVELY, WE COME FULL CIRCLE. EACH
LAP OF LIFE COMPLETED ALLOWS PASSAGE FOR
ANOTHER LAYER TO BUILD UPON.

Appreciate or Perish

GIVE THANKS FOR EVERY FRUIT THAT YOU ARE
GIVEN. THE FRUITS OF LABOR AND LIVING POP
UP AND FADE AWAY, ALWAYS EXPRESS
GRATITUDE FOR HOW YOU ARE NOURISHED. WE
NURTURE OURSELVES BY ACCEPTING THAT
WHAT WE SEE IN ANY GIVEN MOMENT, IT IS NOT
ALL THAT THERE IS. BE GRATEFUL AND KNOW
THAT YOU ARE PROVIDED FOR.

YOU ARE RARE

Rarity is universal, for we all spring forth from the same ether. My gorgeous flower, you are loved most infinitely.

Believe

WHATEVER IT IS THAT SPEAKS TO YOU, BELIEVE
IN IT. FIND THAT UNIQUE ESSENCE OF WHAT
MAKES YOU FEEL MOST ALIVE. ALLOW
YOURSELF THE FREEDOM TO EMBRACE THE
MAGIC.

Be Comfortable

TAKE COMFORT IN KNOWING THAT YOU ARE
ALREADY PREPARED FOR WHAT COMES NEXT.

LET THE PURITY OF YOUR HEART SET THE
INTENTION FOR THIS NEW BEGINNING.

WITH RENEWED CLARITY,
MAKE ROOM FOR EXPRESSING AND ACCEPTING
YOURSELF IN ALL WAYS.

IT IS IN EMBRACING OUR EVERY DYNAMIC
COMPLEXITY THAT WE WHOLLY CONNECT WITH
PEACE IN THIS HUMAN FORM.

Be Softer

SOFTER.
IT IS THE ONLY WAY
TO LIVE AND EXPERIENCE THE GIFTS OF BEING
ALIVE. SOFTER.

WE ARE OBSERVING
THE MIRACLE OF BEING.

EMBRACING ALL THINGS PRESENT.

SOFT NOW.

QUIET IS THE JOY AND LOVE OF LIFE.

LET WHISPERS OF WONDER SPEAK TO YOU.

STEP LIGHTLY.
YOUR WALK IS BRIEF BUT ABUNDANT.
LET THE SOFTNESS COMFORT YOU.

DIVE INTO FEARS AND ANXIETIES.
LEARN THEM.
EVOVLE THEIR FUNCTION.

BE THOUGHTFUL AND DELIBERATE.
LEARN TO BE SOFTER,
SO THAT YOU MAY LIVE A LITTLE MORE FULLY.

Be Free

EXPRESS YOUR TRUTH
BY KNOWING YOUR TRUTH.

IT'S THE ONLY WAY TO FREEDOM.

LET GO OF WHAT YOU THINK IS RIGHT,
SO THAT YOU MAY BECOME REACHABLE.

FIND WAYS TO TURN PAIN INTO LOVE.
YOU ARE FREE TO SEE EXACTLY WHAT YOU
NEED COME TO PASS.

Radiate

SOMETIMES, AS YOU WALK THRU HARD
THINGS, YOU ARE CALLED TO BE THE ONE
HOLDING THE LANTERN. WITH
INTEGRITY, BECOME THE BEACON THAT UNVEILS
THE PATH WITH LIGHT.

To Be Nourished

=

Maintenance

HUNGER AND FORTIFICATION ARE CYCLIC,
NOT ONCE AND DONE.

CYCLE WITH THE INTENT TO MAINTAIN A
NOURISHED HOMEUSTASIS.

THERE IS BALANCE IN

Receiving what you need.

Signal for Receiving

Sometimes, "tough" seems to be going around. I'm positive that it's contagious.

Here's the thing, when you can see and accept that there are many less than desirable aspects of life and circumstance swirling around, but also see all the good, nourishing potential that exists with it, you're a step ahead.

Receiving what we need requires our willingness to usher that in. Steeped in the balance of all things life & love, we steel ourselves into a form that is more than capable of digestion surprises and disappointments because we allow what we need to make its way to us anyway.

On the brink of transforming shifts and stimulation, the centered individual is always well cared for, no matter the shape or tone of the day at hand.

Our time for larger receiving will come, and when it arrives, we will be plenty well-nourished to wield it in line with our authentic confidence and values.

If we want to receive, we have to create space for it. We permit ourselves to be human and to grow through our growth. This is a function of balance. AS we learn more about ourselves and what balance means in our lives, we must realize something pivotal: There is a difference between 'function' and spiritual balance. Only as you become fully integrated into yourself and your connection with the rest of the world can the two concepts merge into the same.

The Let Go List

Control
Obsession
Fear
Material wants
Clutter
Compulsion

What's your Let Go List look like?

"Don't find your balance from a place in your head" "Instead find guidance from the messages of your body."

-Deborah Adele

Throughout our lives, we all vacillate between our points of balance. To invite change to flow through us, we must first let go of the tendency to hold on so tightly to that which no longer serves us.

Deep breaths.

Clear Focus.

Let Go.

Allow lightness and liberation to thrive.

Release all to which you cling in safety.

No more holding back.

Vibrate with Life

WE SHARE A SINGULAR PULSE.

EACH HEARTBEAT VIBRATES WITH
ALIVENESS, SPEAKING HARMONICALLY OF THE
EXISTENCE OF LIFE WITHIN EVERY
CONNECTION.

LINK UP TO THE WORLD WITH YOUR
BEAUTIFULLY UNIQUE RHYTHM, CASTING
INTENTION UPON YOUR EVERY ATTENTION.

Allow the dark and the light, the fast and the slow, the hard and the soft. Resist the farce of duality and separateness.

Choose To Be Whole

PROTECT YOURSELF WITH LOVING-KINDNESS.
BE ATTENTIVE AND AFFECTIONATE.
BE MODERATE IN ALL EARTHLY THINGS.
BLEND THE SEEN AND UNSEEN INTO HARMONY.

Pay Attention

FIRMLY ON THE GROUND,
ROOTED IN PROTECTIVE EMINENCE,
KNOW THAT YOU TO RADIATE DIVINITY.

SPINNING AROUND IN CONSTANT MOTION ARE
WE, ON A ROCK FLOATING IN INFINITY.

MAKE TIME FOR GAZING.

Invite Balance

FEAR NOT THE LIGHT NOR THE DARKNESS, FOR
BOTH NURTURE YOUR EVOLUTION. WHEN YOU
MUST DALLY, TARRY ALONG WITH PROFOUND
AFFECTION. MEET STRUGGLE WITH PATIENCE
AND ALWAYS SLEEP ON THE DIFFICULT, SAVING
PIVOTAL DECISIONS FOR THE BRIGHT, CLEAR
LIGHT OF MORNING.

YIN & YANG IN UNISON

BALANCE ISN'T FOUND IN THE BINARY.

WE CULTIVATE IT IN THE SWEEPING, SWAYING
DANCE THAT EMBRACES THE WHOLE FULLNESS
OF OUR LIVES.

AS WE DANCE THROUGH LIFE, WE TOUCH UPON
EVERY SHADE, LAYER, AND TONE THAT
PRESENTS ITSELF TO US.

YOU ARE THE DANCER, AND YOU ARE
BEAUTIFULLY WHOLE IN YOUR EVERY STEP.

CHANGE FLOATS ON THE WIND.
WHERE IS IT WHISKING YOU TODAY?

Aim only to emerge on the other side of any situation transformed.

HONOR THE CHANGES THAT BREED YOUR EXPANSION, FOR, WITHOUT STRUGGLE, THERE IS NO GROWTH TO THE PERPETUALLY UNCHALLENGED.

Allow the unknown to things to appear, and embrace them with interest.

EXPLORATIVE DISCERNMENT IS A BETTER AGENT OF PEACE THAN JUDGMENT OR DISCRIMINATION CAN EVER BE.

Accept the Dance

HONOR THE PATH IN BEING LESS RESISTANT.

LIFE HAPPENS AS A DANCE.

STEPS CHANGE.

TEMPOS RISE AND FALL.

WE CHOOSE TO EITHER FLOW OR SCURRY.

MAY WE CHANGE AND GROW SO THAT WE MAY
IMPROVE AND RISE AGAIN.

RESIST NOT THE VISIBLE, NOTICEABLE
CHANGES ON THE DANCE FLOOR.

WHAT IS THE DANCE TRYING TO EBB YOU
TOWARD?

Take plenty of walks, for there are many paths ahead.

LET EACH PIECE OF THE PATH UNFOLD TO YOU. STEP WITH LOVE AND CONVICTION. STEER YOURSELF FAITHFULLY IN THE WAYS OF IGNITING KINDNESS. IN YOU, RESIDES A BRIGHT TESTAMENT OF WHAT IT IS TO BE FORMED OF STARDUST.

Pack Lightly

RELISH LUXURY
IN THE SAME WAY AS YOU WOULD POVERTY.

THROUGH UNATTACHMENT,
WE DEVELOP EQUAL FONDNESS FOR ALL.

CARRY NO PENCHANT FOR FAVORITES, FOR,
IN THIS LIFE, WE CEASE TO LIVE IF WE CLING.

STEEPED IN THE CYCLICALS OF
PILGRIMAGE, DISCIPLINE YOURSELF TO PICK UP
ONLY THAT WHICH IS MOST RESONANT.

CARRY ONLY THAT WHICH IS TRULY YOURS.

Rest

VIBRANCY GROWS WITHIN, ONLY ONCE WE TIRE
FROM HABITS OF EXHAUSTION. REST IN
UNCERTAINTY. BREATHE IN BEING. WHATEVER IS
HAPPENING, LET IT HAPPEN WITH EASE.

This dance is a gift that evolves naturally into all the spaces, through which our life will lead.

Can you believe in how loveable you are?

CAN YOU KNOW WITHOUT ANY DOUBT HOW
LOVED AND FULL OF LOVE THAT YOU ARE?

CAN YOU DO THIS LONG ENOUGH TO TAKE YOUR
POWER BACK?

HOW CAN YOU CARRY THIS WITH YOU AND USE
IT AS FUEL TO CREATE SUBSTANTIAL AND
LASTING CHANGE THAT VIBRATES FROM WITHIN?

In examining and discovering the more profound levels of self, you grow more prepared and capable of finding all the people and things that fit just right.

LIVE GENTLY IN THE PROCESS OF BRINGING YOUR LIFE BEAUTIFULLY INTO AUTHENTIC ALIGNMENT.

Nurture the way all
things migrate full circle.

Spiral upward on the
staircase of being.

SHOWER YOURSELF WITH LOVE

Keep Exploring.

EXPLORE ALL THAT YOU ARE DRAWN TO. IN
TIME AND TUNE, FLOW INTO YOUR BEING.

THERE IS RICHNESS IN

Reflection

Rich Reflections

Sometimes, being ruthless with your discernment is the kindest, most loving step that you can take in the process of shedding your old layers. "What is important to me NOW? What work is most meaningful?"

Take a moment and observe how you can ruthlessly examine your discernment, with love. There is nothing hostile about this ruthlessness; it's designed to be thorough. To witness your internal discourse and insight, to reflect it clearly, neutrally, and unapologetically, takes practice.

You can do this because you know that clutching and hanging on to 'old stuff' is a hindrance to your highest self. Playfully, question your discernment often enough to clean up and clear away everything that is no longer serving you.

You are free to clear whatever you need, to shed old skins, and to fully pursue the tasks of work and life at hand today. In deep, honest reflection, the slate is cleared.

You, my Sweet, are the sentinel to your experience in this life.

LET NOT THE EGO MUDDY THAT WATERS MEANT TO FLOW YOUR FORWARD. HOLDFAST FOR PEACE.

THAT Thing

It Happened.

(Past-tense)

IT'S OVER NOW.

I HAVE TO REMEMBER TO LET IT GO.

IT WAS ONE STIMULUS IN MY LIFE.

IT DOES NOT DEFINE MY WHOLE LIFE.

ACCEPT Dissolve

WHO WAS I THEN?

HOW DID IT REFINE ME?

WHAT WAS THE LESSON?

WHERE AM I NOW?

WHAT ABOUT IT CAN I BE THANKFUL FOR?

We don't need to rush or force all the wonderful things for which we aren't quite ready.

Trade Surviving for Thriving.

IT ISN'T AS BIG OF A LEAP AS YOU THINK, BUT IT DOES REQUIRE A COMPLETELY DIFFERENT MINDSET.

SURVIVAL STRATEGIES ARE A FUNCTION OF OUR BASIC HUMAN PROGRAMMING. THRIVING IS A CONSCIOUS CHOICE TO FLOURISH, DEVELOP, AND GROW. FIRST AND FOREMOST, IT'S AN ATTITUDE.

CAN YOU MAKE THAT ADJUSTMENT NOW?

"It's Complicated"
is a copout.

WHATEVER IT IS, UNCOMPLICATED IT.

WHEN WE MAKE THINGS MORE ARDUOUS THAN
THEY HAVE TO BE, MORE DIFFICULT THAN THEY
ARE, AND FALSELY ASSUME THAT THEY ARE AS
CONVOLUTED AS THEY MAYBE FEEL, WE ARE
GETTING IN OUR OWN WAY.

KEEPING IT SIMPLE IS THE SOLUTION THAT
CONQUERS THE EGO'S SELF-WILL RUN RIOT.

How am I showing up in
the world that illustrates
my sacred self-trust?

When we're thriving, positivity and perspective take center stage. It doesn't mean that we don't encounter obstacles or have to work hard. It just means that we're connected, joyful, and making progress in a state of gratitude.

TO THRIVE, WE MUST MAKE CALCULATED ADJUSTMENTS TO OUR LIVES, THOUGHTS, AND THE BEHAVIORS THAT RING TRUE TO WHO WE ARE, FINE-TUNING WHAT'S RIGHT, AND KICKING EVERYTHING LESS THAN DESIRABLE TO THE CURB.

What is complete?

What is percolating?

What wants to grow?

SEND EQUAL PARTS LOVE AND ACCEPTANCE TO
WHAT IS GLOWING AND WHAT IS GROWING.
YOU HAVE SPACE AND YOU HAVE TIME.
GLOW AND GROW WITH ALL YOUR SHINE.

Take Pride in Your Every Act of Progress.

IT IS SEPARATING YOU FROM CONFUSION.

Observe Your Self-Connection

WHERE CAN MY LIFE TRAVEL, IF I CONTINUE
DOING WHAT I AM DOING TODAY?

WHAT IS MY WHY?

WHAT AM I GRATEFUL FOR?

AM I BEING TRUE TO MY VALUES?

WHY NOT?

IS MY TRIBE A POSITIVE INFLUENCE?

DOES MY LIFESTYLE PROMOTE MY WELLBEING?

DO I CARE MORE ABOUT HOW MY LIFE LOOKS OR
HOW IT FEELS?

SAYING No

SAYING "NO" ISN'T DISLOYAL.
IT ISN'T RUDE.

WHEN WE LEARN TO LIVE OUR TRUTH IN THE
ACTIVE APPLICATION OF OUR BOUNDARIES, WE
CIRCUMVENT SITUATIONS THAT BREED
ADDITIONAL GUILT, SHAME, & RESENTMENT.

#AINTNOBODYGOTTIMEFORTHAT

#SAYNOWITHLOVE

SORRY
Not Sorry

Sometimes that's Appropriate

ARE YOU ALLOWED TO SET BOUNDARIES?

ARE YOU ALLOWED TO HAVE LIMITATIONS?

TO HAVE A DIFFERENT OPINOIN?

TO ACT IN WAYS THAT SUPPORT YOUR LIFE
VIEW AND VALUE SET?

F.O̶M̶.O

WE'RE NOT BEATING OURSELVES UP ANYMORE,
REMEMBER?

#SELFLOVESTARTSHERE

STOP SCROLLING, COMPARING, AND GETTING
STUCK IN ALL THE NEGATIVE SELF TALK THAT
GOES INTO OVERDRIVE WHEN YOU'RE LOOKING
AT ALL THE PRETTY, FLUFFY THINGS FLOATING
THROUGH OTHER PEOPLE'S LIVES.

BE HAPPY FOR THEM AND THEIR BLESSINGS.
IDENTIFY AND BE GRATEFUL FOR YOUR OWN.

EVERYONE LIVES IN A BUBBLE OF GIVE AND
TAKE. IT'S NOT JUST YOU.

DON'T FEAR MISSING OUT ON WHAT OTHER
PEOPLE GET AND GET TO DO.

EMBRACE WHAT YOU GET TO DO INSTEAD.

Ever Forward

YOU WERE MADE TO GROW AND FLOW. USHER IN
THE ABUNDANCE THAT IS YOURS. FEED ONLY
THE THOUGHTS THAT STEER YOU TOWARDS
WHAT BECKONS FROM THE DEEP.

Walk, Rest, Repeat

EVERY STEP EMANATES WITH PURPOSE.
DESTINATIONS ARE ONLY PRETTY PITSTOP.

WE'RE ON A MUCH BIGGER JOURNEY
THAN THE MIND CAN SEE.

WISDOM GROWS IN THE SPACES WHERE
INTENTIONS AND IMPRESSIONS ALIGN WITH THE
CLARITY.

PRACTICE UNBIASED EXAMINATION.
WALK, REST, REPEAT
EXPERIENCE, ENJOY, RELEASE.

SANCTION YOUR EVERY INQUIRY TO BE THUS.

THIS IS HOW WE DIVE DEEPER.

THERE IS
TRANSFORMATION IN

Evolving

Evolve

Very little transforms on purpose,
and yet here we are.

How do you capture a moment? A release? A receipt? The subtleties of evolving can seem elusive, and yet, it's our responsibility to soak them into the fullest, but why?

Our evolution is the story of how our inner essence migrates through this fantastical life of nature, relationships, and being. We've accepted that nothing will remain static, so we have agreed to embrace all these transitions most mindfully. Amidst this journey, we evolve best, not by rushing, but by paying attention to the slowing down.

The human lens of perception is like a kaleidoscope—Color, changeable, and revolving. As we evolve into new versions of ourselves, our preceptory vision transforms as well.

We don't learn to trust
ourselves by being in
perpetual motion.

You're Not Stuck

IT IS POSSIBLE YOU'RE A BIT DISCONNECTED.

LET GO OF ACCUMULATED DEFENSES.
GET GROUNDED.
CENTERED.
CALM.

EVEN THE BITE OF LOVE LOST, SINGED, OR
STUNG HOLDS LESSONS AND
OPPORTUNITIES. LOVE IS A NATURAL WAY.

OPEN UP AND INVITE IT IN.

MARINATE IN YOUR DEVOTION.

BE STEERED BY THE FLOW OF LOVE'S
RESOUNDING MESSAGES, AND NEVER CEASE TO
LET LOVE RADIATE TOO AND FROM YOU.

REOPEN THE GATES.

Evolve

EVOLVE FROM EVERY EXPERIENCE. THE GOOD,
THE BAD, AND THE UGLY ARE BUT OUR OWN
FLEETING OPINIONS OF THE OCCURRENCES AT
HAND.

Sparks of you rain down everywhere. The qualities of your composition cultivate unmatchable joy.

believe

It is an honor to know
you.

Progress Transcends Perfection

IF YOU MUST SEEK, SEARCH FOR PARADISE, NOT
PERFECTION. OBSERVE THE TRIALS OF THOSE
WHO'VE GROWN SLAVES TO
FALSEHOOD. SERENITY IS AT HAND, HELD
WITHIN, AND ACCESSIBLE AT ALL TIMES.

IF YOU MUST BE BUSY, BE BUSY LIKE A
BEE; WORK IN SERVICE, CONTENT WITH OR
WITHOUT A GOAL, AND IN FLAWLESS RHYTHM
WITH YOUR HIGHER PURPOSE.

Stoke The Fire

SOMETIMES YOU WALK INTO FIRE WILLINGLY,
OTHER TIMES IT HAPPENS REPETITIVELY.

IS IT A LESSON BEING REVISITED? IS IT A
DESIRE FOR SOMETHING LACKING?

SOMETIMES YOU WALK WILLINGLY INTO THE
FOG, ACCEPTING THAT YOU CAN'T SEE WHAT
LIES AHEAD.

REASON DOESN'T ALWAYS DELIVER YOU WHERE
YOU MOST NEED TO GO.

INSTEAD OF SEARCHING OUT
SHORTCUTS, MAKE YOUR WAY SLOWLY ONTO
THE PATH AT HAND. TAKE THE CLEAR
WAY, LONG THOUGH IT MAY BE, SLOW THOUGH
IT MAY SEEM.

JOURNEY ONLY WHERE YOUR FEET ARE MEANT
TO TREAD.

BLAZE BRIGHTLY TOWARD THE LIGHT THAT
CALLS YOU.

Be Soft

OPEN YOUR HEART IN FAITH.
THIS IS THE WAY TO HEALING WHAT ONCE
WOUNDED US.

SYMPTOMS DISINTEGRATE AND LOSE THEIR
HOLD WHEN WE CAN RECONCILE SPIRIT IN THE
HARMONY OF LOVE.

IN MANY WAYS, WE GRAPPLE WITH BLINDNESS.
THE PAST PAINTS PICTURE WE BELIEVE AS
TRUTH, SO NEVER STRIVE TO OVERCOME.

LET YOURSELF OPEN AGAIN,
IN THE LENS OF LOVE.

OPEN UP TO A NEW STORY.

EVOLVE TO UNRAVEL THE CONFUSION THAT
CLOUDS OUR INNATE SERENITY.

Laugh

LEARN TO LAUGH
LIKE IT'S GOING OUT OF STYLE!

DON'T TAKE YOURSELF SO SERIOUSLY.
LIFE CAN BE AS SILLY OR STRENUOUS AS WE
CHOOSE TO MAKE IT IN EACH MOMENT.

LET LAUGHTER LIGHT YOU UP,
EVEN WHEN YOU WANT TO CRY.
DISPEL EXCESS ENERGY WITH GLEE.

DON'T TAKE IT ALL SO SERIOUSLY.

CRACK A SMILE,
AND FEEL THE RELEASE OF ENDORPHINS START
TO FLOW.

BREAK DOWN WHEN YOU NEED TO.
THEM LAUGH IT ALL OUT.

LEVITY IS ABOUT KEEPING YOU LEVEL.
NOT EVERYTHING IS TEAR-WORTHY.

GIGGLE TILL IT HURTS SO GOOD.
LIFE IS FUNNY-
SO PERMIT YOURSELF TO LAUGH.

Let it be

MANY THINGS WILL UNFOLD.

RECOGNIZE THAT CAUSATION, WORTH, AND
MEANING MAY SOMETIMES SEEM OBSCURE.

PERHAPS, THE TIME IS NOT YET FOR YOU TO
HOLD SUCH UNDERSTANDINGS, AND EVEN IF
THAT TIME NEVER COMES, IT WAS AS IT WAS
SUPPOSED TO BE.

SO IT IS.

Do What Feels Right

WHAT YOU UNDERSTAND AND WHAT YOU
INSPIRE ARE TWO DIFFERENT THINGS, INDEED.

THEY ARE CONNECTED, AND YET,
YOUR FULL UNDERSTANDING OF THAT BRIDGE
MAY BE UNNECESSARY.

DO WHAT FEELS MOST RIGHT WITHIN YOU,
PAUSING NOT TO DEMAND AND GRIEVE THOSE
THINGS WHICH ARE USELESS IN LIFE'S ABILITY
TO FLOW FORWARD.

Walk With Resonant Direction

WALKING WITH YOUR RESONANT WISDOM IS A
PROCESS OF AUTHENTIC LIVING.

TAKE THE TIME THAT IT TAKES TO TAP INTO
THE STILLNESS.

SOAK UP THE RHYTHM THAT RADIATES FROM
WITHIN.

EMBODY YOUR VIBRATION AT ITS PUREST.

Suffer no Folly

THE FOLLY OF THE EGO STANDS BETWEEN US
AND WHAT WE FEEL DIRE TO SEE MENDED.

TO SOOTHE ALL MALADIES, WE CONNECT WITH
THE DIVINE. IN CONNECTION, WE ACCEPT OUR
LIMITATIONS AND OPEN OURSELVES TO
MIRACLES BEYOND OUR CURRENT
UNDERSTANDING.

Leaning In

COURAGEOUSLY, WE LEARN TO SHARE OF SELF
IN WAYS THAT SURPASS ALL PREVIOUSLY
PERCEIVED LIMITATIONS.

WE LET GO OF THE FEAR OF JUDGMENT AND
ALLOW INSIDE ALL OF OUR PUREST PARTS TO
SHINE.

FROM OUR INNER LIGHT, WE GLOW IN
DEDICATION.

SHARING IS THE ACT OF VULNERABILITY THAT
BRIDGES US TO ALL THAT SEEMED IMPROBABLE
BEFORE WE WERE READY TO RECEIVE IT.

IN OUR HUMILITY, WE OPEN UP
AUTHENTICALLY, AND IN THAT, THE TIDES OF
OUR MOST LOVING CONNECTIONS TO THIS
WORLD ARE SET FREE.

Courage

LET GO ALL THE NARRATIVES OF CHILDHOOD.

EVERYTHING THAT SERVED BEFORE HAS SHED
AWAY, ALREADY SERVED ITS PURPOSE.

COURAGE MANIFESTS UPON SOLID
CONVICTIONS. YOU DON'T HAVE TO BE ANY
WHICH WAY ANYMORE.

YOU CHOOSE WHAT STORY YOU ARE LIVING IN.

BE BRAVE ENOUGH TO EXPRESS
YOUR CONVICTIONS, DESPITE ANY VARYING
OPINIONS AND JUDGMENTS.

LIVE EFFORTLESSLY IN KNOWING THAT YOU ARE
BEING LED.

FOLLOW ONLY THE LOVE AND BELIEFS OF YOUR
HIGHEST SELF WITH COURAGE.

Raise Your Vibration.

PROTECT YOUR ETHEREAL SOURCE ENERGY.

CLEANSE IT OF ALL ACCUMULATED RESIDUE.

RESET.

RECENTER.

RISE UP.

EVEN WHEN EVERY OTHER CHOICE SEEMS
EASIER, CHOOSE THE CLEAN, RESONANT
VIBRATION OF PEACE.

PEACE WITHIN AND PEACE WITHOUT.

PEACE PAINTS LIGHT UNTO THE WORLD,
AND VIBRATES WITH THE GREAT EQUALIZER OF
LOVE.

Reach out into
the dreamscape
for the textures
of your
migration.

SPLENDID IS THE WORK OF
BRINGING YOUR INTERESTS TO
LIFE.

And now, we arrive at an ending. Whether it was just a little or a lot that you needed to delve into with Natural Resonance, I'm so delighted that you did.

May you find what you need, exactly as you need it; comfort, inspiration, and perspective. As you tap into your vital energies often, may you excavate and tap into all the beauty of your soul. Whenever you need a friend, reach here in quiet moments and allow the words and graphics to uplift you.

As you honor, all the sacred spaces within yourself, may your journey refine and unwrap you beautifully as you go. End what is ending with integrity & recognition, and center yourself as you prepare to begin once again.

"Celebrate endings
—for they precede new beginnings."

- **Jonathan Lockwood Huie**

THE DIVINE LIGHT
WHICH SHINES IN ME
SENDS LOVE AND
COMPASSION TO YOU.

LIKE ALL THE
UNDERTONES AND
OVERTONES OF YOUR
LIFE,

MAY YOU NATURALLY
STEP INTO BALANCE.

WISHING LIGHT, LOVE, &
LEVITY TO ALL!

Namaste.

-*Meg*

Visit me anytime at:
lightloveandlevity.com

References

Dale, Cyndi (2009) The Subtle Body; An Encyclopedia of your Energetic Anatomy.

Goldman, Jonathan (2018) The Power of Sound Healing

Ludlam, Julia (2020) 25 Inspirational Quotes to Celebrate New Beginnings. Country Living. https://www.countryliving.com/life/g30337217/new-beginnings-quotes/?slide=2

Sweatt, Lydia (2017) 13 Uplifting Quotes About New Beginnings. Success.com Accessed September 5, 2018 at https://www.success.com/13-uplifting-quotes-about-new-beginnings/